高级口语教程

主　编　侯爱华　董勇英　杨　跃

参　编　高　鹏　张兰兰　戴玉霞

　　　　李长安　许小花

西安电子科技大学出版社

内 容 简 介

　　本书旨在提高学习者运用英语进行商务活动的能力，从而接轨其职业发展需求。全书包括 16 个单元，内容涵盖公司概况、产品服务、办公艺术、跨文化交际等多个商务活动主题，教学资源丰富，教学设计严谨。每单元以"五分钟商务活动"为导入，然后围绕主题进行相关语言和技能的学习，进而以角色扮演和案例分析为载体，实现学与练的有机结合。同时，辅以范本，引导学习者学会正确得体地使用商务英语。另外，在每单元末尾，我们编写了"背景知识"和"会话技巧"。前者专门介绍与该单元主题相关的文化亮点或特色事物，以期激发读者的阅读兴趣，进而自主学习，并从中终身受益。后者则注重交际意识和技巧的培养，为接轨职业发展提供有力支持。

　　本书既适用于学习者自主学习，也可以作为教师授课的素材；既可作为大学涉外专业的商务英语教材，也可作为大学英语选修课和行业培训教材。同时，书中丰富的主题、真实的商务活动案例，也可为其他英语使用者提供有效的参考，助力沟通，提高商务交际能力。

图书在版编目(CIP)数据

高级口语教程 / 侯爱华，董勇英，杨跃主编. —西安：西安电子科技大学出版社，2019.6
ISBN 978-7-5606-4003-7

Ⅰ. ① 高… Ⅱ. ① 侯… ② 董… ③ 杨… Ⅲ. ① 英语—口语—教材 Ⅳ. ① H319.9

中国版本图书馆 CIP 数据核字(2019)第 096272 号

策划编辑	邵汉平	
责任编辑	邵汉平　徐忆红	
出版发行	西安电子科技大学出版社(西安市太白南路 2 号)	
电　　话	(029)88242885　88201467	邮　编　710071
网　　址	www.xduph.com	电子邮箱　xdupfxb001@163.com
经　　销	新华书店	
印刷单位	陕西日报社	
版　　次	2019 年 6 月第 1 版　　2019 年 6 月第 1 次印刷	
开　　本	787 毫米×960 毫米　1/16　印　张　7.5	
字　　数	144 千字	
印　　数	1～1000 册	
定　　价	28.00 元	

ISBN 978-7-5606-4003-7 / H

XDUP 4295001-1

如有印装问题可调换

前　　言

为了满足高等院校学生和广大学习者提高商务英语技能的需求，弥补接轨职业发展、提升沟通的英语书籍的匮乏，编者根据教育部具体的教学目标设计和编写了《高级口语教程》。该书实现了工具与人文的有机统一，激发读者的学习兴趣，提高其运用英语进行商务交际的能力，从而实现毕业就业无缝接轨。

《高级口语教程》旨在充分调用学生已具备的英美文化基本知识和英语表达能力，引导高等学校学生学英语、重应用的理念更新，重点培养商务英语交际的能力，提升学生的职场竞争力。本书的主要特色如下：

将英语交际活动的真实内容引入课堂教学，体验真实的商务英语交际活动。在英语教学中，交际活动与英语教学脱节一直是困扰教师的难题。本书以 5 分钟商务活动引入主题，启发性的问题均以真实的商务活动为参照，使学生身临其境，在领略文化的同时，学习语言、提高交际能力。

语言表达与样本示范相得益彰，为提高交际能力打下基础。以主题为载体，词汇、核心句型的学习与讨论相结合，系统而循序渐进地讲解交流技能，夯实交流要点，解决盲点和难点，为提高交际能力打下基础。

从学生的需求和兴趣出发。选取的主题反映了大部分学生的需求和兴趣，可激发学生进行进一步学习和探索。

适用面广。本书既适用于学习者自主学习，也可以作为教师授课的素材。教师还可以根据学生自主学习的情况选取符合学生需求的主题，与学生进行讨论。同时，本书丰富的主题、真实的商务活动案例，也可为其他英语使用者提供有效的参考。

本书包括 16 个单元，内容涉及公司管理和商务活动，语料紧跟时代发展，内容新颖，信息丰富，更为关注经济社会的热点问题。其主题涵盖多个商务活动环节，如公司概况、产品服务、办公艺术、跨文化交际等，每单元围绕主题进行相关语言和技能的学习，注重引导学生学会正确、得体地使用商务英语。另外，在每单元末尾，我们编写了"背景知识"和"会话技巧"，专门介绍与该单元主题相关的文化亮点或特色事物，以期激发读者的阅读兴趣，开阔视野，进而自主学习，并从中终身受益。

编　者

二〇一九年四月

What is in the units?

Five-minute activity You are offered a realistic business situation and an inspiring question by which you can discuss the topic of the unit and exchange ideas about it.

Useful expressions This section focuses on language and communication skills. It provides you with the language you need in the realistic business world in the form of references. Accomplish the task, and you will master the language and communication skills involved.

Models for reference This section will come to your aid when it is difficult for you to participate in the discussion. It provides you with the models you can follow in the realistic business world in the form of models. Refer to the models, and you will broaden your horizon and grasp the essence in communicating in the realistic business world.

Case study This section is linked to the business topic of each unit. The realistic business problems and situations will enable the learners to practice their speaking skills based on the languages and communication skills provided previously while working through this unit.

Class time for topic-related discussion This offers you opportunities to further practice the language and communication skills you have developed concerning the topic, build your confidence in English speaking and improve the accuracy and fluency through interesting role-play activities.

Key sentences You will learn important new sentences which you may use in the discussion of the topic and thus increase your business language.

Further reading The further reading is linked to the business topics of each unit. You will read authentic articles on the topics, develop your reading skills, broaden your horizons and further your understanding of the topic.

Background information You are offered a direct examination of the foreign culture, customs and language.

Conversational skills This section focuses on delicate and realistic business situations. To survive in the competitive global business world, not only should you develop language for skills such as negotiating, decision making and team-work but numerous other essential business communication skills as well.

Contents

Contents

Unit 1   Dealing with Problems

Five-minute Activity

"Huston, we have a problem."

It goes beyond doubt that we have undergone some problems in our daily life. Present your problems with order and give details.

Useful Expressions

Word Bank: Problems

faulty goods	dodgy digital content	shoddy services
cable TV provider	airline /car services	changes at work
inefficient receptionist	the place where you live	space problems
money problems	difficult people	

Models for Reference

Inefficient Receptionist

The bad experience at the reception leaves me with a very negative impression on the company. First, I was kept waiting in the reception area for over 15 minutes (three occasions). Second, I was sent to the wrong part of the building for an appointment (two occasions).

Space Problems

Our company pays a lot of rent for an office in the CBD. There isn't enough room for all our staff. Everyone has to be crowded into small offices. We really need a spacious office. The only way out is to move outside the city center as soon as possible.

Case Study

How can we tackle the complaint?

Useful Expressions

Answering the phone	Getting through
Hello, this is Fly & Sharks.	Can I speak to Maria Smith, please?
Good morning, Monica Gomez speaking.	Is Mr. Porter available now?
	Can he call me back, please?
Apologizing	**Stating the problem**
I'm very sorry about that.	I've got a problem with…
I'm sorry to hear that.	There are some problems with…
Asking for details	**Giving details**
Can you give me some more information?	There's a piece missing.
Which model is it?	It's the wrong item/part/model.
	The invoice is incorrect.
Offering solutions	**Closing a conversation**
We can offer you a refund.	Are you available/Can I reach you at this number all day?
I will talk to the manager.	Thanks for your help.
We can send you a new one.	Thank you.

Models for Reference

Practice with the expressions you have learned in this unit and refer to the Model Dialogue if necessary.

Model Dialogue 1

Freda: Hello, Cara Telecommunications.

Dustin: At Last … I was just about to hang up. I've been on the phone for almost half an hour going through various options, one of which I wanted!

Freda: I do apologize for the wait, sir. How may I help you?

Dustin: I've been waiting in all day for an engineer to come and repair my line. He was due to come at 9 o'clock this morning, and it's now 4 in the afternoon. I telephoned at 11 o'clock, and one of your operators promised to get back to me within the hour, but she hasn't. I've wasted my whole day waiting around, and what's more, I still can't receive any calls.

Freda: I'm very sorry, can I have your number and I'll look into it immediately.

Dustin: Yes, it's 04332687796.

Freda: OK, I'm going to contact the engineer that has been assigned to the job to find out what happened. And I have to put you on hold for a while.

Dustin: Pleases don't disappear. As I said, it took me half an hour to get through in the first place.

Freda: Don't worry, I'll come straight back to you. One moment ... Right, I'm afraid he's been delayed on another job. He apologizes for not calling you. He normally works until 5 p.m., but he promises to work late this evening to fit in your job. He can be there by 6 p.m.. Will that be convenient?

Dustin: No, It would not. I am engaged this evening.

Freda: I quite understand. In that case, I'm going to reschedule him for another day. When would it be convenient for you?

Dustin: Tomorrow morning 9 o'clock.

Freda: Ok, I'll see what I can do. Please just bear with me for a moment while I speak with him again ... Right, tomorrow morning at 9. Meanwhile, I'll divert any calls coming into your office number onto your mobile phone until your line is repaired. Will that be acceptable to you?

Dustin: I suppose so. When can you do that?

Freda: If you'd like to tell me your mobile number, I can get that activated immediately.

Dustin: OK, the number is 201 258 1908. Thanks for your help.

Model Dialogue 2

Stella: Hello, Stella Perez speaking.

Patrick: Hello, Ms. Perez. This is Patrick Ross from HairGlow Cosmetics.

Stella: Hello, Ms. Ross. How can I help you?

Patrick: Well, it's about the CN108 order. I'm afraid we need the order a little earlier than expected. Can you supply from the stock?

Stella: OK, I'll see what I can do. Since we have a large backlog this season, I'm afraid

NOTES

I'll have to talk to a few people here before confirming the change. I'll get in touch with you later. Will that be acceptable to you?

Patrick: Yes, of course. But I really do need to know as soon as possible.

Stella: Yes, I quite understand. I'll try to get back to you within the hour. Did you leave your number with our secretary?

Patrick: Yes, she made a note of our office number and you can reach me at this number all day long.

Stella: I've got that.

Patrick: I would really appreciate that. Thanks for all your help.

Class Time for Topic-related Discussion

You are unhappy with the order placed with the HWM Company. There are two problems. First, the sweaters are of wrong color and size. Second, you have ordered 5000 not 500. Telephone the company's sale representatives and figure out the solutions.

Practice these key sentences.

■ I'm afraid he's not in his office right now.

■ Sorry, I think you've got the wrong number.

■ I do apologize for the wait, sir.

■ How can I help you?

■ I'm very sorry. Can I have your number and I'll look into it straight away?

■ I quite understand.

■ If you'd like to tell me your mobile number, I can get back to you later.

Further Reading

How to express an effective complaint?

The airline lost your baggage. The restaurant served the wrong order. The taxi driver overcharged you. Sometimes things go wrong and you have to do something about it! Use these tips when you want to make an effective complaint in English.

Be polite! The way to complain is to act business-like and important. No matter how unfair the situation is, it's best to phrase your complaint politely. Suppose your hotel laundry ruined your favorite shirt, make a polite but firm request to see the manager. When the manager comes, ask his or her name. And then state your problem and what you expect to have done about it. It's advisable to use indirect language to sound more polite. For example, you can start a complaint with "I'm sorry to bother you" to put the listener who may have heard many complaints that day at ease. "Can you help me with this? My sweater came back from the laundry still with coffee spot." Everyone would much rather be asked to do something than told! So try to phrase your complaint as a request for help.

Act decently. If you act like someone who expects a fair request to be granted, chances are it will be granted. People are often treated the way they expect to be treated. Don't put on airs and say, "Do you know who I am?" You should be firm in making your complaint, but shouting or acting rude will get you nowhere.

Be business-like and stick to the point. Don't talk too much about how you tried to fix the problem but couldn't.

Besides what have been mentioned above, sometimes you're treated so badly that there's no time for being polite! You can use these very direct phrases when a problem is beyond compromise: "This is unacceptable," "Please fix the situation immediately," or "I demand a refund."

Things not to Miss

1. Background information

Collect call. It is a telephone call in which the calling party wants to make a call at the called party's expense, so it is also known as a reverse charge call in the majority of the English-speaking world. With the introduction of computer-based telephone dialing equipment, it is now possible to place a collect call without using an operator, which is called automated operator services (AOS) as opposed to Home Country Direct (HCD). Other forms of paid communication, such as telegrams and mail, could also be sent as "collect". The movie *The Parent Trap* can be referred to as to this kind of call.

2. Conversational skills

Think twice before you leap. Do not aggravate the situation by taking sides with or carrying tales back to any one party when receiving the complaint of the customer. What you should focus on is to solve the problem rather than talking about the responsibilities. Here comes the example:

The purchasing manager from the Simon Crystal has ordered a consignment of forks from your company. Unfortunately, your employee made a wrong order. What should you do when you receive the complaint?

First, apologize and show understanding. "I am really sorry about that. I do apologize…/ I can totally understand how you feel." Soothe the client so that we can get down to the business.

Second, offer to help. "How can I help?" "I will look into it right now and give you a reply in two weeks." It's great to show that you will pay attention to this matter. The period "two weeks" is long enough for you to get a clear idea of what has happened and think about an effective solution. Never make any promise too hastily and then go back on your words!

Third, make suggestions. After you've figured out the whole situation, solutions can be put forward. "Perhaps we could…" "Would it be possible to …?"

NOTES

Unit 2　Inquiries

Five-minute Activity

What should be stated in an inquiry and the answer?

Make an inquiry for the product you are interested in and give the answer to the inquiry.

Useful Expressions

Word Bank: Delivery Terms

EWX	FRC	FOR	FOA	FAS
FOB	CFR	CIF	DOP	CIP
EXS	EXQ	DAF	DDP	

Models for Reference

An Inquiry

July 7, 2018

Dept. of International Sales

Vermeer Manufacturing Company

P. O. Box 200/3668 New Orchard Rd.

Pella, Iowa 50219

U. S. A.

Dear Sir or Madam,

Product Catalogue and Price List Requested

During our visit to the Office Trade Fair in Jakarta last month, our attention was drawn to your comprehensive selection of paper products. We are currently looking for a new office supplier with a wide range of paper products, computers and desktop accessories, as well as a variety of writing supplies.

Please provide us with quotes for the goods listed on the enclosed inquiry sheet, giving your prices FOB San Diego including 3% commission. Please also state your earliest delivery date, your terms of payment and discounts for regular purchases.

We look forward to hearing from you soon.
Sincerely,

Joseph De Haan
Commercial Manager
Encl.: inquiry sheet

An Answer to an Inquiry

July 26, 2018

MARIAN   IMP. & EXP. CORP.
268, Sharon Rd.
Delfi Orchard
Singapore 0923

Dear Mr. Haan,

Re: Product Catalogue and Price List

Thank you for your letter of July 7, 2018 and the enclosure requesting quotes for our products and services. We are pleased to inform you that our company offers a very broad range of paper products and office supplies at a very competitive price. We are confident that we can meet all your stationery, electronic and writing needs.

As requested, we are submitting our quotations in triplicate and wish for you to place your order with us as earlier as possible because we have a large backlog. You will also find a comprehensive product catalogue as well as other information about our company. Our regular purchases in quantities of not less than five gross of individual items we would allow you a discount of 2%. Please note that our terms of payment are by irrevocable L/C at sight.

If you would like further information or a demonstration of any of our electronic goods, I would be happy to arrange for a representative to come to you whenever it is convenient. Alternatively, you can visit our showroom during regular opening hours.

We await your decision.

Sincerely,

Sander Monroe
International Orders and Deliveries Manager

Case Study

When you are looking for a new printer supplier, how can you establish trade relations and make the inquiries?

Useful Expressions

Establish trade relations	Polite requests
Our attention was drawn to your products at Guangzhou Trade Fair.	Please let us know if you can also supply from stock.
You were recommended to us by Daniel Marshall.	

We sincerely hope to establish business relations with your company so as to promote the bilateral trade.	Please state the earliest date on which you can deliver.
Inquiry I am writing to inquire about your special offer on printers. Could you please send us a copy of your current price list? Do you supply from stock?	Please quote your lowest prices. Please inform us of your terms and conditions.
Thanks Thank you for your letter of June 16 inquiring about our products. We were pleased to receive your inquiry. Thank you for your inquiry dated June 16. Thank you for the interest you have shown in our products. We are pleased to inform you that we stock a broad range of paper products. We are happy to confirm that we can meet all of your stationery needs. We are happy to supply you with the information you requested. Unfortunately, we are not able to meet your electronic needs. We regret to inform you that we do not supply any electronic goods.	**Enclosures** As requested, I am enclosing our current price list. Please find enclosed a copy of our latest catalogue. Enclosed you will find three stationery samples. We are pleased to enclose the samples you requested.

Models for Reference

Practice with the expressions you have learned in this unit and refer to the Model Dialogue if necessary.

Model Dialogue 1

Daniel: Our attention was drawn to your products at Guangzhou Trade Fair. This is our inquiry, Mr. Zhao.

Zhao Zhiqin: Thanks.

Daniel: As the corporation specializes in importing printers, we'd like to have your lowest quotation CIF Toronto.

Zhao Zhiqin: Oh, well, please tell us the quantity you want so we can work on the offer.

Daniel: All right, but could you give us an indication of your price?

Zhao Zhiqin: Sure. This is our FOB quotation sheet.

Daniel: Are the prices on the list firm offers?

Zhao Zhiqin: All the quotations are subject to our final confirmation.

Daniel: OK, thanks. As to the quantity we intend to order, we'll let you know tomorrow.

Zhao Zhiqin: See you tomorrow then.

Daniel: Bye.

Model Dialogue 2

Colin: I understand that you're interested in our electronic products, Mr. Zhang.

Zhang Zhiming: Yes. Your company has been recommended to us by one of our suppliers, The Paper & Things.

Colin: This will certainly offer us an opportunity to develop bilateral trade. Our company handles a great variety of electronic products. What particular items are you more interested in?

Zhang Zhiming: Oh, here is our inquiry. Please have a look.

Colin: Sure. Thanks.

Zhang Zhiming: We hope you'll quote us your most attractive price CIF Suzhou. If your quotation is competitive, we are ready to conclude substantial business with you.

Colin: OK. We'll get it prepared. Let's discuss business in detail this afternoon.

Zhang Zhiming: Very good. See you this afternoon.

Colin: Goodbye.

Class Time for Topic-related Discussion

Suppose you are the purchasing manager of Vermeer Import Corporation. Make an inquiry for the Chinese black tea. This should include a brief introduction to your company, how you know the other company, your specific requirements and eagerness to establish trade relations.

Practice these key sentences.

- This corporation specializes in importing teas.
- We wish to introduce ourselves to you as a state-operated corporation dealing exclusively in various kinds of Chinese black tea.
- Your firm has been recommended to us by the Chamber of Commerce in New York.
- We read your advertisement in *The Washington Post*.
- We would be pleased to receive your catalogue.
- We would like to know if you stock Chinese black tea

Further Reading

When writing an inquiry letter, you are to ask for more information concerning a product, service or other information about a product or service. These letters are often written in response to an advertisement that we have seen in the paper, a magazine, a commercial on television when we are interested in purchasing a product, but would like more information before making a decision. Inquiries are also written to ask for business contact information to develop new business.

Remember to place your or your company's address at the top of the letter (or use your company's letterhead) followed by the address of the company you are writing to. The date can either be placed double spaced down or to the right.

Following are some other important points to be included:

- The start: Dear Sir or Madam

To whom it may concern—(very formal as you do not know the person to whom you are writing)

- Giving reference: With reference to your advertisement (ad) in...

Regarding your advertisement (ad) in ...

• Requesting a catalog, brochure, etc.: After the reference, add a comma and continue—..., would (could) you please send me ...

• Requesting further Information: I would also like to know ... Could you tell me whether ...

• Signature: Yours faithfully—(very formal as you do not know the person to whom you are writing)

Things not to Miss

1. Background information

San Diego　a coastal city of the Pacific Ocean in the very Southwest of California, approximately 120 miles (190 km) south of Los Angeles and immediately adjacent to the border with Mexico. With an estimated population of 1,345,895 of 2013, San Diego is the eighth-largest city in the United States and second-largest in California. San Diego is the birthplace of California and is known for its mild year-round climate, natural deep-water harbor, extensive beaches, and recent emergence as a healthcare and biotechnology development center.

2. Conversational skills

You are on the phone call for a long time and you really want to hang up. How to do it politely? Even if you are crazy, you still should stay cool and be polite.

You can tell the truth when you can. For example, "Pepper, I have to get back to work," or "Dad, dear, I will call you back. My kids are crying now."

You should also be firm, especially at work if you're needed elsewhere. "Thanks for calling, but I have a speech to give right now and I must go." To show your sincerity, you can provide the caller with a better time to call, if you're so inclined. Or provide another option for communication, such as an e-mail address, a P. O. Box or a better time to contact, like "Can I call you back in 15 minutes?"

Another case that you may want to hang up is that the person is a telemarketer, someone that may be harassing you over the phone. You can give the caller one warning: "I am hanging up in 30 seconds; call our support center if there's another issue."

Tact is the art of making a point without making an enemy. Just try to be the best one in talking with your etiquette and you will make it!

Unit 3   Quotes and Orders

□□□□□□□□⇨

Five-minute Activity

How can you re-open the conversation with the customer who showed interest in your product but didn't ask for any more information?

How can you place an order on the products that you are interested in?

Useful Expressions

Quotes	Order
overall price	Enclosed please find our order. / Our order is enclosed.
components of the price	
terms and conditions	We would like to place the following order.
payment terms or schedule	We herewith order the following items.
delivery	We require the goods urgently.
packing	We would be grateful if you could deliver as soon as possible.
postage	
expiry date	Please let us know when we can expect the delivery.

unit to place an order	warehouse	to purchase
to be available	supply	in stock
showroom	to be on hand	estimate
door-to-door shipping	to depend on something	location

Models for Reference

A Quote

August 04, 2018

Pame Factory

641 N Broad St

Middle Town, DE 48790

Dear Mr. Smith,

We heard that your company is interested in the office stationery at the Toronto Trade Fair. We are pleased to quote as follows:

1 Marcom X Photo Color Printer $699

1 box Plain White Standard Business Envelopes $8.29

1 case White Copy Paper $41.99

1 ream Glossy Photo Paper $29.99

These prices include shipping and handling. Delivery can be made from stock and we will allow you a 4% discount on items ordered in quantities of 30 or more. There is an additional cash discount of 2% on the total cost if payment occurs within 15 days from the date of invoice.

We hope you will find these terms satisfactory. Don't hesitate to call me if you have any questions.

Sincerely,

Steve Monroe, Orders and Deliveries Dept.

Placing an Order on the Phone:

Jane: Hello, this is Jane Tegal from Accelerator Co. calling. May I speak to Mr. Mitchell?

Mitchell: Hello Ms. Tegal, this is Arthur Mitchell.

Jane: Hello, I'd like to place an order for a number of your Millennium desk units.

Mitchell: Certainly. How many are you interested in ordering for purchase?

Jane: Quite a few. Do you have many available in the warehouse?

Mitchell: We keep a large supply in stock. There's also a showroom with quite a few on hand. It shouldn't be a problem.

Jane: Well then. I'd like 75 units by the end of the month. Could I get an estimate before place an order?

Mitchell: Certainly, I'll have it for you by the end of the day.

Jane: What does the estimate include?

Mitchell: Estimates include merchandise, packaging and shipping, duty if required, any taxes and insurance.

Jane: Do you ship door-to-door?

Mitchell: Certainly, all shipments are door-to-door. Delivery dates depend on your location, but we can usually deliver within 14 business days.

Jane: Thank you for your help.

Mitchell: My pleasure. You can expect an e-mail by 5 this afternoon.

Case Study

What elements should be reckoned with when we are dealing with order changes?

Useful Expressions

Word Bank:

purchase order	delivery	ship
be due	shipping terms	shipping process

Models for Reference

Practice with the expressions you have learned in this unit and refer to the Model Dialogue if necessary.

Model Dialogue

Jane: Julia, please come to my office. I just received a revised purchase order from one of our customers. Remember the order we received from Colors House two weeks ago?

Julia: The one for a lot of 500 oak wood windows?

Jane: Yes, that is the one. Did we start production on it yet?

Julia: I do not think so since we do not have to make delivery until the twentieth of this month, another fifteen days.

Jane: Good. I just received a revised order from its Purchasing Department. They want pine wood instead of oak wood.

NOTES

Julia: We have already ordered the oak wood from Lumber House. It will cost us more if we put in a change of order now.

Jane: Don't worry. Colors House is willing to pay an extra twenty-five percent for the change.

Julia: It is OK then. When do we have to ship the order? Is it still due on the twentieth?

Jane: No, they gave us extra time to fill the new order. It is not due until the twenty-fifth of the month now.

Julia: Did they change the shipping terms? Do we still have to deliver the order, or will they come here to pick it up?

Jane: We still have to take care of the shipping process, and it is still going to Chicago.

Julia: Then I do not have to make any shipping changes other than changing the pickup date. I had better give a copy of this new order to our Production Department. They need to be aware of the change.

Jane: Thanks for your help, Julia.

Julia: You are welcome, Jane.

Class Time for Topic-related Discussion

You are now contacting a potential customer you just met in the exhibition. Give an oral introduction to the products he is interested in. Price of products included. Find a partner to be the customer who negotiates with you and finally places orders.

Practice these key sentences.

- Please send us the undermentioned goods.
- We should be grateful for delivery by 26th September 2018.
- Please confirm receipt of the order.
- Your prices are not competitive enough.
- Please submit a quotation for a substitute.
- We will require two weeks to process your order.
- Delivery will be made by 6th July 2018.

Further Reading

You attitude

"You attitude" means looking at things from the readers' (or business partners') point of view, emphasize what your partner wants to know, reflect and focus on the needs, interests and concerns of your partner. This works well in positive and neutral situations.

To be specific, you can focus on what the reader receives or can do. In positive situations, like placing order, you can use "you" more often than "I" or "we". For example, expression like "We will give you a discount on the future purchases." focuses on what the writer can give. If it is changed into "As a regular buyer, you can get a 10% discount when you place future orders with us", you will protect the buyers' ego and keep a good relationship.

You can also refer to the readers' request or order specifically. Compare "We will ship your order this afternoon." This generic "your order" may confuse the reader. While "The 5,000 pieces handbags you ordered on March 20 will be shipped this afternoon and should reach you by April 20.

In any case, don't make your message all about "me" or "us". If you're trying to persuade your readers to buy a product, emphasize what's in it for them.

Things not to Miss

1. Background information

A payment is the transfer of an item of value from one party (such as a person or company) to another in exchange for the provision of goods, services or both.

The simplest and oldest form of payment is barter, the exchange of one good or service for another. In the modern world, common means of payment include money, check, debit, credit, or bank transfer, and in trade such payments are frequently preceded by an invoice or result in receipt. However, payments may take the form of stock or other more complicated arrangements.

In 2005, an estimated $40 trillion globally passed through some type of payment system. Roughly $12 trillion of that was transacted through various credit cards, mostly the 21,000 member banks of Visa and MasterCard. Processing payments, including the extending of credit, produced close to $500 billion in revenue. In 2012, roughly $377 trillion passed through non-cash payment systems. This led to total account and transaction revenues close to $524 billion.

2. Conversational skills
How to keep a conversation going?

It's quite often that when we are talking to someone we've just met, the conversation is staling. Breaking the silence and keeping the conversation going can avoid the awkward.

Finding your favorite topics with new people would make easy conversational topics for you and build a beautiful relationship with the new people. Then you can ask open ended questions. In this way, you can get the other person talking. These questions can be followed up by more information, instead of simple "yes" or "no" answers. Similarly, when offered some information, you can use "what", "where", "why", "how", "when" "who" questions to keep the conversation going. For example, "I went to the movie." Instead of "yes", you can further ask, "Where is the movie theater?" "Who did you go with?"

Besides, you can express agreement or nod to show you are a sympathetic listener. When another person ends the talking, you can say "well," followed by repeating what (s)he just said. People love to know that you're interested in what they have to say, so if you show some interest and agreement, they'll want to talk to you even more. Expressions like "Oh! That's interesting...", "Hmm, I've never heard of that", "Hum, cool!" are very flattering to them.

If you do these, you'll make conversations far more interesting, with natural ease, avoiding all awkward silence that might prevent you from meeting the right friends.

Unit 4   Making Offers and Bargaining

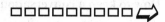

Five-minute Activity

You are at a flea market in a foreign country and are attracted to a set of antique silver cutlery. Now make your offer and bargain with the vendor.

Tips on how to bargain well

Bargaining is appropriate sometimes, but not all the time.

Find out what locals pay.

Determine what the item is worth to you.

Don't show too much enthusiasm for whatever you're eying.

If an item is worth more to you than you paid for it, it is acceptable that you paid more than the local.

Start 25% to 30% lower than the first offer.

Get a friend or spouse to go with you.

Find flaws.

Don't be afraid to walk away from an item, even one that you love.

Be ready to spend a long time bargaining.

Impress the merchant with your knowledge.

Seek a discount for cash.

Don't insult the seller.

Models for Reference

Sample Bargaining (1)

Buyer: How much is it?

Seller: That'll be $100, sir.

Buyer: I'll give you $70.

Seller: How about $90?

Buyer: How about $75?

Seller: Fine. I'll be willing to settle for $85.

Buyer: And I can settle for $75.

Seller: $80?

Buyer: $75.

Seller: I will take $78 dollars.

Buyer: And I will give you $76.

Seller: $78 dollars is my final offer.

Buyer: And $76 is mine.

Seller: $77?

Buyer: OK!

Seller: $77 it is, then, ma'am.

Sample Bargaining (2)

Buyer: What's the unit price for 500 pieces?

Seller: That would be 120 yuan.

Buyer: That's a bit more than we expect. Can you come down a bit?

Seller: I'm afraid that's the best we can do. Actually, we can consider lowering the unit price if you can order more. 500 is really not a big order.

Buyer: Then, how many pieces do you think is the minimum order?

Seller: If you can order more than 1000 pieces, we are willing to go down to 115 yuan.

Buyer: 115 yuan per piece for 1000 seems a bit high to us. I happen to know that you went down to 110 yuan per piece for another company last week. How about you drop the price to 110 yuan and we order 1000 pieces?

Seller: Well, I think we have no problem with that.

Buyer: OK! Now we've got a deal!

Case Study

How should a negotiator start the negotiation appropriately?

Useful Expressions

Let's negotiate the price.	Our opinion on the issue is very simple.
We offer you our best prices, at which we have done a lot business with other customers.	Let us have your rock-bottom price.
	That sounds very impressive.
I hope this meeting is productive.	The price is unreasonable.
We'll come out from this meeting as winners.	I'm sure the prices we submitted are competitive.
Let's compromise.	We can work out the details next time.
The longer we wait, the less likely we will come up with anything.	May I suggest that we continue tomorrow?
	Let's dismiss and return in an hour.
I'm sure there is some room for negotiation.	That will eat up a lot of time.

Models for Reference

Practice with the expressions you have learned in this unit and refer to the Model Dialogue if necessary.

Model Dialogue 1

Carter: Hello! Mr. Lee, welcome to China! I am Judy Carter, sales manager. It is a great pleasure to meet you.

Lee: Nice to meet you, too, Mrs. Carter!

Carter: I'm afraid that our costs for the product won't go down much, even with future business.

Lee: So, you mean you'll stick to what you are proposing.

Carter: We could take a cut on the margin. But 20% would cut our profit margin. Maybe we can compromise. How about 12%?

Lee: That a big change from 20%. 12% are beyond my negotiating limit.

Carter: I don't think we can change it now.

Lee: But Mrs. Carter, it is really beyond my limit. Maybe we can try to come up something else.

Carter: We hope so, too. We propose a deal. For the first 12 months, we give you a discount of 15%, and then the discount goes back to 12%?

Lee: Mrs. Carter, I can't bring those numbers to my office.

Carter: I'm afraid it's about the best we can do.

Model Dialogue 2

Zhou: I think we all know each other, so let's get started.

Brown: Okay, well, we've had a look at your computer game and we think it has potential.

Zhou: That's fantastic. Then it's a matter of getting down to business and talking about costs, the terms of payment, the marketing involved...

Wang: We'd like to turn to the marketing later.

Brown: Yes, we can come back to that if we're satisfied with the financial side of things.

Zhou: Okay, let's talk about money then. Frankly, we think that 40 percent of the retail cost is a fair price.

Brown: That would be $25 per unit for an order of 20,000. I'm afraid that is a bit high.

Zhou: What makes you say that?

Brown: To start with, your game "Return of the Warrior" is based on a movie. If the movie isn't a hit, we're left with a product we can't sell.

Fox: I agree to a certain extent, but remember, the first one, "The Warriors", was a huge success. It broke all of the box office records.

Wang: Yes, that's true. I saw it too and thought it was terrific. But the second one "The Knight's Quest" was dismal. There are no guarantees here.

Zhou: On the one hand, I can understand your concern. On the other, the Warrior series has a huge following. The risk is minimal.

Fox: The fans will buy the products no matter how bad the movie is.

Wang: Still, I have my doubts. $25 a unit is just too much. We might be prepared to buy at $15 a unit.

Zhou: With a production cost of $5 per unit, we'd be left with a margin of $10. That's not good business for us.

Brown: You may have a point here and it's true that the margin isn't too wide, but you have to understand our position. We are willing to take a risk, but only a limited one.

Zhou: Well, how would you feel about $20 per unit?

Wang: But with the transportation costs, it's still too much.

Zhou: As long as you agree to $20, we would be prepared to cover the transportation costs.

Brown: What time frame are we looking at here?

Zhou: I think this will need to be looked at later. There are more pressing issues at hand. Let's try to come to a decision on the price first. Then, we can proceed onto other issues.

Brown: I'm afraid I can't give you the final word on this right now. I'll have to consult my boss first. However, provided that you take over the transportation costs, $20 per unit will probably be acceptable.

Zhou: I might as well run this by our headquarters too.

Class Time for Topic-related Discussion

You and your colleagues are going to attend a meeting to negotiate the prices of your products with your clients. Prepare together with your colleagues by having a mock meeting. Some of you would represent your own company and the others would represent your clients' company.

Practice these key sentences.

- I need to talk to my team about this.
- I don't think my boss would go for that.
- This issue will be addressed later.
- There are more pressing issues at hand.
- I can't speak for everyone on this.
- We can offer you a discount of 12 percent.
- I cannot give you the last word on that.
- The best I can do is to agree to extend the warranty period.
- I will have to consult my boss on this.

Further Reading

Business negotiations: making the first offer

The way you open business negotiations influences the entire process, from the initial offer to the final agreement. For first-time negotiations, especially between different cultures, these opening moments are even more critical.

Negotiators should ask themselves three questions when preparing their opening offer: Who should make the first offer? Should the offer be high (if you are exporting) or low (if you are importing)? What should you do if your opening offer is rejected?

While some negotiators recommend letting the other side open the discussions, others suggest that making the first offer gives you a tactical advantage. Actually, these suggestions are simplistic and they generally apply to one-time business deals. Doing business in the global arena is a long-term prospect, where personal relationships are essential. Skilled and experienced negotiators create a favorable atmosphere that has a positive impact on the tone, and progress of negotiations, as well as the final agreement.

For fruitful negotiations, the opening offer should be clear and positive, stress mutual benefits, imply flexibility, demonstrate confidence and promote goodwill.

The opening phase is the time to identify the other side's underlying needs and your common interests, and emphasize the mutual benefits to be derived from reaching agreement. In the initial stage of the discussions, you should be prepared to set aside differences of interests and potential obstacles that could derail the negotiations. Your first offer should be viewed as fair and reasonable. The other party may require justification to support your proposal. You should be in a position to provide it. Overall, the opening offer should be on the higher side to give you room to maneuver and at the same time protect your margins. Research has proven that negotiators starting with high aspirations generally obtain higher outcomes than those with lower or more modest goals. As a rule, importers do better if they start with low offers, while exporters get better results with high openings.

In view of the above findings, sellers may be tempted to start high and buyers to begin low to maximize their outcomes. However, as every deal is different, both sides should consider each new negotiation as unique, and should be extremely careful in the preparation of opening strategies. Skilled negotiators bear a number of factors in mind when planning their opening offer: cultural norms prevailing in the target market;

competition in their line of business; and whether they are seeking repeat orders over the long term. What's equally important is how badly they need the deal and whether they have other business alternatives.

Things not to Miss

1. Background information
Box office

A box office is a place where tickets are sold to the public for admission to an event. People may perform the transaction through a wicket, a hole in a window or a wall, or at a countertop. Also, the term is frequently used in the context of the film industry, indicating the amount of money a particular production, such as a film or an opera show, receives. Usually, box office can be measured by the analysis of the number of tickets sold or the amount of money raised by ticket sales. The analysis of these earnings is very important for the arts industries and can often arouse fans' great interest. Some complain that if the arts industries only focus on profit, the quality of films as an art form would be ignored to some extent. However, analysis of the financial success of films is very important for the funding and production of films in the future.

2. Conversational skills
How to make the first offer

Most of us think, in a business negotiation, we should let the other side make the first offer. Actually, when it comes to negotiation strategies, it is not always wise to wait for the other party to make the first offer, to suppress emotions during bargaining, or to reveal too much too early. Instead, you should make the first offer because of the power of anchoring.

In making the first offer, you gain an advantage by deciding the starting point to which the other side must respond. The only times when it makes sense to wait for the other side to make the first offer are when you have information that gives you significant advantage in the bargaining or when you really believe that the other party dramatically values the object of the exchange at a much higher price than you do.

Your first offer should be "extreme." How "extreme" should it be? You must be as aggressive as possible while remembering not to cross a line that would prompt the other side to shut down negotiations and walk away. And if you can't risk an impasse or you think the benefit you might receive is not worth the time it takes to negotiate, a first offer should be on the low side.

People don't usually think emotions can be used strategically. Actually, emotions can be powerful pieces of information. The belief that a poker face is a key to success in negotiations, and that the rational negotiator is always the unemotional negotiator is not necessarily true. In some cases, negotiators who displayed anger during the process created more value than those who were unemotional.

Besides, negotiators must also always bear their greatest weapon in mind: the ability to walk away. If you are facing a bad deal, you can choose to leave.

Unit 5   Logistics

□□□□□□□□⇨

Five-minute Activity

What do you think is the most important factor in logistics, time, service or cost?

What are the responsibilities of a logistician besides managing the transportation?

Useful Expressions

Word Bank:

keep track of	delivery	warehouse
net weights	gross weights	unloading
items	a nonstop flight	actual time of departure
bulk cargo	certificate of origin	preliminary inspection

Models for Reference

Karen: What are you in charge of for your company?

David: I work with the head of logistics, managing the flow of goods in and out of my company, which offers a very good deal on office supplies.

Karen: Sounds cool! Generally, what affect the deliveries?

David: Well, there are weather delays and shipment delays due to reduced production. Sometimes, larger packages are delayed because of a bottleneck at the distribution point.

Karen: Is there any way around these days?

David: Well, we often work with delivery services such as UPS, Fed or DHL for your most urgent shipping. They guarantee door-to-door deliveries within 48 hours.

Karen: Are they expensive?

David: Yes, they're very expensive and cut into our bottom line.

Case Study

How can a logistician manage the supply chain?

Useful Expressions

Word Bank:

package delay	bottleneck	distribution	timeline
get back on schedule	shipment	urgent	shipping
door-to-door service	bottom line		

Models for Reference

Practice with the expressions you have learned in this unit and refer to the Model Dialogue if necessary.

Model Dialogue

Susan: David, can I talk with you for a moment?

David: What can I do for you, Susan?

Susan: I'm concerned about the delay we're experiencing with the supplies we ordered one month ago. But they haven't arrived yet.

David: We're doing everything to get back on schedule.

Susan: Could you give me an approximate timeline?

David: Well, let me have a check. Um, the truck just has pulled them in the warehouse in Illinois. Laura, who is responsible for the delivery, will upload them tomorrow and ask the driver to send the boxes to you then. So, they will arrive at the warehouse of your company the day after tomorrow. I'll keep track of the delivery. I'm really sorry for all the troubles caused.

Susan: Thank you. Hope they will arrive as you told, or this delay will kill our business!

Class Time for Topic-related Discussion

Work with your partner. Study the following situation and then act out the telephone conversation sensitively.

You have ordered delivery of a new laptop computer. When you track the order on

the Internet, you find that it has gone from UK to Hong Kong. But you live in China. Telephone the supplier to find out what's happening.

Practice these sentences.
- Mike was tracking orders when the first shipment came in.
- They've been traveling to Hawaii every year for twenty years.

Further Reading

Reverse logistics: definition and a brief history

Though the conception of Reverse Logistics dates from long time ago, the denomination of the term is difficult to trace with precision. Terms like Reverse Channels or Reverse Flow already appear in the scientific literature of the seventies, but consistently related with recycling (Guiltinan and Bwokoye, 1974; Ginater and Starling, 1978).

During the eighties, the definition was inspired by the movement of flows against the traditional flows in the supply chain, or, as put by Lambert and Stock (1981), "going the wrong way" (see also Murphy, 1986, and Murphy and Poist, 1989).

In the early nineties, a formal definition of Reverse Logistics was put together by the Council of Logistics Management, stressing the recovery aspects of reverse logistics (Stock, 1992), "…the term often used to refer to the role of logistics in recycling, waste disposal, and management of hazardous materials; a broader perspective includes all relating to logistics activities carried out in source reduction, recycling, substitution, reuse of materials and disposal."

The previous definition is quite general, as is evident from the following excerpt, "the role of logistics in all relating activities". Besides that, it is originated from a waste management standpoint. In the same year, Pohlen and Farris(1992) define Reverse Logistics, guided by marketing principles and by giving it a direction insight, as follows, "…the movement of goods from a consumer towards a producer in a channel of distribution."

Kopicky et al.(1993) defines Reverse Logistics analogously to Stock(1992) but keeps as previously introduced by Pohlen and Farris(1992), the sense of direction opposed to traditional distribution flows:

"Reverse Logistics is a broad term referring to the logistics management and disposing of hazardous or non-hazardous waste from packaging and products. It includes reverse distribution...which causes goods and information to flow in the opposite direction of normal logistics activities."

At the end of the nineties, Rogers and Tibben-Lembke (1999) describe Reverse Logistics stressing the goal and the processes the logistics involved:

"The process of planning, implementing, and controlling the efficient, cost-effective flow of raw materials, in-process inventory, finished goods, and related information from the point of consumption to the point of origin for the purpose of recapturing value or proper disposal."

The European Working Group on Reverse Logistics (1998-), puts forward the following definition, which we will use in this chapter:

"The process of planning, implementing and controlling backward flows of raw materials, in process inventory, packaging and finished goods, from a manufacturing, distribution or use point, to a point of recovery or point of proper disposal."

This perspective on Reverse Logistics keeps the essence of the definition as put forward by Rogers and Tibben-Lembke (1999), which is logistics. We do not, however, refer to "point of consumption" nor to "point of origin." In this way, we give margin to return flows that were not consumed first (for instance, stock adjustments due to overstocks or spare parts which were not used) or that may go back to a different point of recovery than the original (e.g. collected computer chips may enter another chain). We employ the expression "point of recovery" to stress the distinction we want to make from pure waste-management activities. Furthermore, we include the "reverse direction" (backward flows) in the definition to exclude what can be considered forward recovery (for instance, when a consumer gives his/her personal computer to the neighbor).

In summary, the definition of Reverse Logistics has changed over time, starting with a sense of "wrong direction", going through an overemphasis on environmental aspects, coming back to the original pillars of the concept, and coming finally to a widening of its scope.

Things not to Miss

1. Background information

Logistics is the management of the flow of goods between the point of origin and the point of consumption in order to meet requirements of customers or corporations. The resources managed in logistics can include physical items, such as food, materials, animals, equipment and liquids, as well as abstract items, such as time, information, particles, and energy. The logistics of physical items usually involves the integration of information flow, material handling, production, packaging, inventory, transportation, warehousing, and often security. The complexity of logistics can be modeled, analyzed, visualized, and optimized by dedicated simulation software. The minimization of the use of resources is a common motivation in logistics for import and export.

Supplier relationship management (SRM) is the discipline of strategically planning for, and managing, all interactions with third party organizations that supply goods and/or services to an organization in order to maximize the value of those interactions. In practice, SRM entails creating closer, more collaborative relationships with key suppliers in order to uncover and realize new value and reduce risk.

2. Conversational skills
How to change the subject with a bridge?

Have you ever wanted to change the subject and talk about something more interesting or relevant? Yes, you have and you can. You don't have to be at the mercy of a bore or windbag. And when your date or interviewer asks questions you don't want to answer, you can deftly change the subject and talk about something else. Media trainers have a name for this conversation technique: bridging.

Once Maharishi Mahesh Yogi (yes, the Beatles' guru), was interviewed on American TV. When the interview got started, the TV host took one look at his guest and blurted, "What do you eat?" Obviously, it was an off-beat question. Maharishi was a man on a spiritual mission. Thousands had attended his lectures in India. He did not come half-way around the world to discuss food. He could have said, "What a silly question!" But that's offensive, not a gracious way to change the subject. Keeping his purpose in mind, *he answered the question he wished he'd been asked.* He launched into his favorite metaphor about the source and nature of life: "Water the root to enjoy the fruit." His answer was very clever and appropriate, indeed. But the best reply would have been something like this, "Many people have asked that question, and what I want to tell you and your viewers is how to enjoy life. It is so much simpler than what you eat. Take this flower for example..."

This technique is called bridging，which means you start with where the other person is and you create a transition, a bridge, to where you want to go. You can try it with job interviewers, long-winded colleagues, boring relatives and friends who can't stop talking about the latest scandal.

If you listen carefully when politicians answer journalists' questions, you'll hear how skilled speakers bend questions to get their point across. And, of course, you can practice your bridging skills. You don't even have to be talking to practice. Just pick a sentence that someone else has just said and mentally bridge to a new conversation topic. Later, when you really need to change the subject, you'll do it smoothly.

Unit 6　Closing a Deal

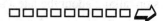

Five-minute Activity

You are the sales manager of your company and your company has just closed a deal and established a long-term relationship with a very famous international company. Now you are at the celebration party with your co-workers and you are going to propose a toast. How would you do it and what would you say?

Tips on how to propose a toast

Think about or write your toast in advance.

Use tidy note if you have any.

Don't forget to acknowledge people who are not present.

Show your emotion.

Make it short.

Don't drink and speak.

Useful Expressions

I now propose a toast to the future cooperation between XXX company and our company.

I'd like to propose a toast.

May I have your attention, please? I'd like to propose a toast.

I'd like to propose a toast to our new friends.

Everybody, I'd like to propose a toast to Stella, the best salesperson of the year.

Here's to you, Stella!

Here is to our friendship/health/success!

We are proud of you!

Models for Reference

A Short Speech with the Toast

Your Honor Mr. Huntington, ladies and gentlemen,

It's our great honor and pleasure to host this banquet in honor of our distinguished guests—Mr. Huntington and his team. Apparently, the contract we signed today has demonstrated Mr. Huntington's determination to further develop the friendly and cooperative relations between our two companies. We greatly cherish this close relationship, and also greatly value the role we play as one of your most important trading partners. I sincerely wish that we could continue to cooperate to ensure a sustained growth in our cooperation of economy, finance and trade. On this delightful occasion, I wish Mr. Huntington and all our guests present tonight good health!

Thank you!

Case Study

What should be paid attention to when closing a deal?

Useful Expressions

I'm glad we could settle that.	We're prepared to sign this.
This is turning out to be a very productive day for us.	Today's negotiations have been very successful.
I want to quickly reiterate the main points.	I think this was beneficial for all of us.
Let's run through today's figures.	I'd like to suggest a toast to our cooperation.
Now is a good time to go over the main points.	Here is to our next project!
I'd like to summarize what we've agreed on today.	Let's call it a deal!
I'm glad to cooperate with you.	Before the formal contract is drawn up, we'd like to restate the main points of the agreement.
This is a fair deal.	We can get the contract finalized now.

Models for Reference

Practice with the expressions you have learned in this unit and refer to the Model Dialogue if necessary.

Model Dialogue 1 (Part 1)

Cook: I'm pleased to say that we got the go-ahead from headquarters for $20 a unit on the condition that you take over the transportation costs.

Jobs: That sounds good. I'm glad we could settle that. This is turning out to be a very productive day for us.

Cook: Okay. That leads us to the next point: the terms of payment.

Johnson: We usually expect full payment within 30 days of delivery.

Williams: Full payment in 30 days. This could be a problem for us. If we agreed to this, it could generate a cash flow problem.

Jobs: I understand the constraints you're under. However, I'd like to reiterate that we, too, are working on a tight budget.

Williams: It's obvious that we all need to compromise on this if we are to close this deal.

Jobs: Of course. What would you propose?

Cook: If you were to give us 60 days, we'd be able to pay the full amount all at once.

Johnson: I fear we couldn't manage this. The financial burden would be too high.

Cook: Well, how about 50 percent after 30 days and the remainder in 60 days?

Jobs: Quite frankly, we're not looking at a big enough sum to justify two payments. Would you consider 100 percent within 45 days?

Williams: That strikes me as a viable solution.

Cook: 45 days. Alright, that's acceptable. I think it's a fair deal.

Jobs: We're glad we could settle this.

Model Dialogue 2 (Part 2)

Jobs: I think that wraps up today's session. Have we forgotten anything? Okay. So, I'd just like to summarize what we've agreed upon today. First of all, we decided to sell our game at a cost of $20 per unit.

Cook: And you also cover the freight and import tax.

Jobs: That's right. We'll cover the transportation costs. You're going to start off with an order of 20,000.

Cook: We'll discuss subsequent orders when we get an idea of how well the games sell.

Jobs: Yes. You're going to take care of the marketing.

Cook: Absolutely. We have quite a few Warrior fans on our marketing team. They'll love this project.

Jobs: That's good to know.

Williams: And finally, we agreed to pay in full within 45 days for the terms of payment.

Jobs: I think we've summed up everything.

Johnson: Yes. It seems to me that we've conducted successful negotiations.

Cook: We're satisfied with the outcome too, and we look forward to doing business with you.

Class Time for Topic-related Discussion

Suppose you are a sales person for smart devices (phones, laptops, accessories, tablets, wearables, etc), please close a deal with the representative from Thailand.

Practice these key sentences.
- I'm glad we could agree on this.
- I'd like to sum up if I may.
- We've been very productive today.
- You could save a lot if you would order a little more.
- If you order in large lots, we'll reduce the price.
- I think we can do that.
- Okay, I think we have a deal.
- So, we've reached an agreement.

Further Reading

Ideas for closing a sales deal

A deal usually consists of several parts: the hatching of the idea by one party, then its conceptual embrace by the other side, and finally—the closing. Closing a deal—because of the prospect that it might fall apart before you get to that point—can put a lump in the throat of any small business owner.

Yet, there are ways to make you a better "closer":

Get more than a verbal "yes": Time is money, but sometimes it is also your enemy. Once you've managed to get your target to agree in principle that you're going to make this deal, move them as quickly as possible toward getting it into writing. That's because into the narrow opening between "yes" and signing on the papers can creep common sales problems like second thoughts, competition or unforeseen events. So if you get a verbal expression of interest or commitment from your client, then move as quickly as possible to a written agreement that hopefully closes out the sales deal.

Create a sense of urgency: Sometimes the other party doesn't seem to be so eager to close the deal. They will be happy to close it—when they can get around to it. Chances are that timing may be much more important to you. So if necessary, you may try to create a sense of urgency to get their commitment, which may require some final concessions to help refocus their attention. This may involve offering a 2% greater discount, or offering a two-year service agreement instead of one-year coverage.

Use the strategy of competition: Sometimes, in order to get the person on the other end of the deal to close it, from time to time an entrepreneur will have to get them to understand that if they don't do the deal with you, you'll do the deal with someone else. Sometimes this involves bluffing, sometimes enhancing the appeal of what you're offering. But if you can convince your client that you're doing something that's going to become powerful, everybody wants a piece of that.

Generate "late-breaking news": During the process of relationship-building and negotiating and beyond, funnel helpful new information to the other side. This might be a story about your business that you've managed to land in the local newspaper, a press release about your new product, the result of a new independent test of your product and service, or one testimonial from an recent customer that you're keeping in your briefcase.

Be prepared to not close: If you measure by the number of potential relationships and transactions that your company pursues, the reality is that most deals don't close. Something unexpected may happen. Maybe there isn't a fit or the timing just isn't right. You must disdain losing any deal and fight hard to land every last one. But you also need to be sober about the percentages—so you can raise them.

Things not to Miss

1. Background Information
Methods of payment in international trade

There are many ways to make and receive payment in international trade. Salespeople must offer their customers attractive sales terms supported by the appropriate payment methods to win sales against competitors. There are three popular payment methods for trade.

1) Letters of credit

Letters of credit is one of the most secure transaction methods available to international traders. An L/C is a commitment by a bank on behalf of the buyer that payment will be made to the exporter, provided that the terms and conditions stated in the L/C have been met, as verified through the presentation of all required documents.

2) Remittance

Remittance includes M/T (Mail Transfer), T/T (Telegraphic Transfer) and D/D (Demand Draft).

Among the three different methods, T/T (Telegraphic Transfer) is the easiest payment method and is usually used when small quantity shipments or samples are transported by air. T/T is also used between buyers and exporters who have already established a mutual trust between them.

3) Documentary Collection

Documentary Collection can be further divided into D/P (Documents against Payment) and D/A (Documents against Acceptance).

A documentary collection (D/C) is a transaction in which the exporter hands over the task of collecting the payment for a sale to its bank, which sends the shipping documents to the buyer's bank together with instructions to release the documents to the buyer for payment. A documentary collection (D/C) is so-called because funds are received from the importer and remitted to the exporter through the banks involved in the collection in exchange for those documents. D/Cs involve using a draft that requires the importer to pay the face amount either at sight (document against payment) or on a specified date (document against acceptance).

2. Conversational skills
Conversational skills for salespeople

Good salespeople endeavor to find a way to make a connection with their customers, and build a conversation based on understanding and trust, which requires a good mastery of some useful conversation skills. These conversation skills include:

Talking knowledgeably about your product or service; asking non-confronting questions to show you genuinely care about what your customer needs; displaying interest and warmth; respecting and adjusting to your customer's verbal style; avoiding bias or stereotyping; offering observations that show you understand; accepting and acknowledging your customer's opinions; watching for and responding to signs of discomfort or boredom; refraining from interrupting or correcting your customer unnecessarily; making small talk to an appropriate degree when it is necessary.

Unit 7   Getting the Meeting Started

Five-minute Activity

What information should be included in a meeting agenda?

Write an agenda based on your answer to the first question.

Tips on how to write an agenda for a meeting

1. Give your agenda a title.
2. Include "who", "where" and "when" information in the header.
3. Write a brief statement of the meeting objective(s).
4. Write a schedule outlining the main elements of the meeting.
5. Allocate time in the schedule for any special guests.
6. Leave extra time at the end of the meeting for Q&A.
7. Check the agenda for errors before distributing it.

Models for Reference

Meeting Agenda 1

Sales meeting

July 15th, 2016, 9:00 AM-12:00 AM

Host: Anna Lee

Attendees: Bob Smith, Anna Lee, George King, Tim Heck, Daniel Miller, Richard Green, Chris Roberts, Billy Carter

Time	Topic	Presenter
9:00 AM -9:15 AM	1. Brief Introduction	Anna Lee
9:15 AM-9:45 AM	2.1 Review of Previous Minutes	Anna Lee

9:45 AM-10:15AM	2.2 Sales Activities	Anna Lee
	3. Break	
10:15 AM-11: 45AM	4.1 Salesperson Success Stories	George King
	4.2 Opportunities and Prospects	Bob Smith
	4.3 Salesperson Success Stories	Chris Roberts & Richard Green

Meeting Agenda 2

Reading Club Meeting Agenda

Date/Time: Tuesday, February 28, 2017,9 a.m. to 11 a.m.

Location: Lucy Jane's house, 345 Denver Street, Hamden, CT 06518

Attendees: Jim Smith, Louis Carter, Julie Moore, Sue Heck, Tiffany O'Connor, Kennedy Burbank

Objective

Weekly discussion of club's book.

This week, it's *The Kite Runner*. Assign leaders to ask discussion questions and have lengthy discussion.

Schedule

9:00—9:15: Welcome; appetizers and cocktails served – Lucy Jane

9:15—9:30: Begin discussion and give overview of the book – Julie Moore

9:30—10:20: Discussion of the book – Julie Moore

10:20—10:30: Introduction of next book, *Final Appeal* – Kennedy Burbank

10:30—11:00: Dessert and wrap-up – Lucy Jane

Roles/Responsibilities

Food set-up: Tiffany O'Connor

Discussion questions: Julie Moore

Desserts: Megan Mark

Case Study

As the chairperson, what preparations should you make before the meeting?

Useful Expressions

Thank you for attending today's meeting. Let's get things under way. Let me bring your attention to the main issues. Let's focus on the main issues. Allow me to set out the main issues for you.	To address this issue, I'd like to call on… To shed some light on this, I'd like to call on… Let's look at the agenda and talk about the first item. The first thing on the agenda is the drop in sales. Without further ado.

Models for Reference

Practice with the expressions you have learned in this unit and refer to the Model Dialogue if necessary.

Model Dialogue 1

David: Susan, I took a quick look at the agenda this morning.

Susan: Oh good. Would you like to make any amendments?

David: No, I think you've covered everything. Have you contacted all the committee members?

Susan: Yes, I was able to reach everyone yesterday.

David: That's great news. So, let's get down to business.

Susan: Certainly, but before we start, I'd just like to mention that the Wilson report isn't finished yet.

David: I see. Well, let's turn to the second item of the agenda then.

Model Dialogue 2

Daniel: If everybody's here, we're ready to begin.

David: Have you had a chance to see the city yet?

Daniel: Ahem ... Well, ladies and gentlemen, I think we should get down to business.

Lucy: Yes. I got a quick glimpse this morning.

Daniel: I'd like to call the meeting to order. Let me begin by welcoming you all to The Giant Whales' headquarters. And a very warm welcome to all the new team members.

David: I think that means me. I'm David, by the way.

Daniel: I'm Daniel Lee. For those of you who don't know, I'm the CEO of GW and I don't see that changing in the near future.

David: I love those introductory jokes.

Daniel: I'm going to be chairing today. This is Collin O'Hara, who'll be taking the minutes.

Collin: That's me… good morning.

Daniel: Let me also introduce you to Lucy Jameson, who is going to present a market analysis, and Lisa Turner, who will present the sales figures.

Lucy: Good morning.

Lisa: Hello.

Daniel: But before we turn to the first item on the agenda, I'd like to mention that our marketing manager, Luke Carter, will not be able to join us.

Lucy: That's unfortunate. I was looking forward to meeting him.

Daniel: He has been called away on urgent business.

Collin: So, I'll put him on the absentees list.

Daniel: I hope you've all had a chance to read through the briefing papers. You'll find a copy of the agenda in front of you.

David: Oh goodness! It looks pretty long. We'll be here all night.

Daniel: Now, as you all can see, we have quite a long list of items on the agenda, so let's try to keep to the schedule. Is there any last minute amendment to the agenda? Good. Let's address the first point then: The review of the latest sales figures. Lisa, could you start us off, please?

Lisa: Certainly. Welcome everyone. Without further ado, let us examine the latest sales figures, a copy of which you will find in the folders in front of you.

Class Time for Topic-related Discussion

Alex was newly promoted, and it's his first time to preside over a meeting, how should he start it?

Practice the key sentences.

■   I think we should get down to business.

- I'd like to call the meeting to order.
- Right, let's begin, shall we?
- I think we should begin.
- Okay, so we're ready to begin.
- On the agenda, you'll see there are three items.
- There are four main points to discuss today.
- Shall we move on to the next item on the agenda?
- Let's turn to the second issue.
- Let's move on to the next point.

Further Reading

How to preside over a meeting

When you're presiding over a meeting, remember what people say in the real estate business: the three most important things are "location, location and location". The three most important things in running a meeting are preparation, preparation and preparation. So the most important thing is you should have an agenda, consisting of just a few notes in front of you to make sure you cover what you want to cover in that meeting even if it's an informal one. Having an agenda will considerably enhance your chances of meeting your objective by coming out of the meeting with what you want. Your prospects of having a successful meeting start with your own preparation.

The following are some other helpful hints:

First, start on time. It sounds basic, but think of the meetings you've been to that didn't start on time. If you allow last night's baseball game to be the first subject of discussion at the table, you have no momentum for a brisk, decisive, productive meeting.

Then, be decisive. You've established what the issues are. Then the two questions for each item are: what action is to be taken, and who's going to do it? If you leave these things vague, there was no point in having the meeting in the first place.

Finally, be firm. Don't let others try to score points off each other or waste time in other ways. You don't have to be the bad guy and chide them. Show them the time and just say, "Sorry, Mike—we've got to move on to the next item." There's no reason for you to be afraid of seeming bossy or brusque. Just relax. If you can run a short meeting and get decisions made, you will earn far more gratitude and goodwill than you would be letting everybody ramble, and then presiding over a failed meeting.

Things not to Miss

1. Background information
Agenda

An agenda may also be called a docket or schedule. It is a list of meeting activities in the order in which they are to be taken up and usually includes one or more specific items of business to be discussed. It may, but is not required to, include specific times for one or more activities. Optimally, the agenda is distributed to a meeting's participants prior to the meeting, so that they will be aware of the subjects to be discussed, and are able to prepare for the meeting accordingly.

In the meeting, as later agenda steps may be dependent upon information derived from or completion of earlier steps in the agenda, the order of agenda items is important. Frequently, agenda items may be fixed or "time boxed" in standard meetings, so as not to exceed a predetermined amount of time. In a meeting, time boxing may not be effective because completion of each agenda step may be important to beginning the next step.

Usually, a typical agenda may be headed with the calendar date, time and meeting venue, followed by a series of points outlining the order of the agenda. Agenda items should focus on the deliverable from each step. Steps on any agenda can include any type of schedule or order the group wants to follow. There are many different agendas used, which just depend on what the group's specific purpose is. The various purposes may include:

Old business or open issues; New business such as specific points to be discussed — this section is where the discussion usually takes place and decisions in the meeting are made; Other issues: a participant may be allowed to raise another point for discussion; Close meeting to include review of key points, discussion of assignments, and confirmation of the next meeting, etc.

2. Conversational skills
Invitation: the art of good questions

What makes conversations flow smoothly?

Conversations flow when they move from topic to topic and speaker to speaker in a way that feels smooth and natural. One of your primary tools for helping conversations flow is the idea of invitation.

An invitation is something you say that communicates very clearly that it is now your partner's turn to talk, and gives a strong suggestion for what your partner should talk about.

For instance, "What did you do today?" is an invitation. It's obvious that you are inviting your partner to speak, and you are giving a clear idea for what they should talk about!

Since most invitations are questions, good questions are what makes good invitations, and vice versa. For a question to be a good invitation, it needs to be open-ended instead of being closed-ended. An "open-ended question" refers to an invitation that allows your partner to talk at length, instead of being limited to a short answer. When you ask a closed-ended question like "Did you have a good weekend?" your partner will likely answer "Yes" or "No." Since you're looking for smooth, flowing conversation, a one-word response is not ideal. But if you ask the same question in an open-ended way, you will give your partner a much better invitation. When you ask "What did you do this weekend?", your partner is free to tell you the full story of their weekend. You're still asking about their weekend, but you're asking it in a way that invites them to share.

If you're not sure what to say next, just throw out an invitation and the conversation will keep going.

Unit 8   Starting the Formal Presentation

□□□□□□□□□⇨

Five-minute Activity

How to grab the attention of the audience in a presentation?

Make a presentation on the top-10 discoveries of the decade/ your favorite movie.

Useful Expressions

Introducing the topic:

Today, I am here to talk to you about…

I would like to take this opportunity to talk to you about…

Today I would like to outline…

Starting presentation	Main-body
My presentation is in three parts.	As I said at the beginning…
My presentation is divided into three main sections.	This, of course, will help you (to achieve the 20% increase).
I'll start with/ I'll begin with/ First I will take a look at…/ talk about…/ examine…/ tell you something about the background…/ give you some facts and figures…/ concentrate on…/limit myself to the question of…	As you remember, we are concerned with…
	This ties in with my original statement…
	This relates directly to the question I put to you before…
	I'd now like to move on to…
	I'd like to turn to…
Please feel free to interrupt me if you have questions.	That's all I have to say about…
There will be time for questions at the end of the presentation.	Now I'd like to look at…
	This leads me to my next point…
	This graph shows you…
I'd be grateful if you could ask your	Take a look at this…

questions after the presentation.

Changing the topic/ speaker:	**Summarizing**
Right, let's move on to…	That brings me to the end of my presentation.
This leads me to my next point, which is…	I've talked about…
	Well, that's about it for now. We've covered…
Now I will pass you over to/ hand over to Max.	So, that was our marketing strategy. In brief, we…
	To summarize, I…

Inviting questions:

Does anyone have any questions?

If you have any further questions, I will be happy to talk to you at the end.

Sample Presentation 1
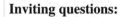

Tim: I'm going to take a look at our budget for next year. May I draw your attention to this pie chart? The pie chart is divided into three parts. It shows a breakdown of our budget in terms of advertising, production and research and development. Can everyone see the chart?

Audience: Yes.

Tim: Good. Here we can see that our budget breaks down to 75 percent for production costs, 10 percent for R&D and 15 percent for advertising. How should we interpret this data? In order to understand this, I'd like to go a little deeper and compare these figures with those of our budget 10 years ago. Here we can clearly see that we are still dedicating exactly the same amount of resources to R&D and advertising.

But the market is changing rapidly and our competitors are taking actions to adjust to the new market. According to the latest data from consultancy, competitors are already investing 20 percent on the R&D. Such higher input in the updating of products certainly will win them more market.

To summarize, we need to strengthen our technology in the future. We will talk about the new solution later today.

Sample Presentation 2

Hi, everyone! Today, I'd like to take this opportunity to talk to you about my favorable movie "Titanic" with Leonardo DiCaprio and Kate Winslet, directed by Cameron.

I will start my presentation from the plot outline and end it with the reasons why I like it so much.

The movie begins with a scene displaying the R.M.S. Titanic in 1912 a few minutes before departing on its Maiden Voyage. The 2200 people are seen waving goodbye for the last time, unknown to them. The endless waters of the Atlantic are seen sloshing as the title is displayed: *TITANIC*. This movie focuses on the romantic tale of a rich girl and a poor boy who met on the ill-fated voyage of the "unsinkable" ship. Jack, the poor boy winning the trip on Titanic during a card game spots. Rose, an unhappy girl on her way to marry her rich fiance. They two fell in love. Their love came to a new level when Rose asked Jack to draw her in the nude wearing the invaluable blue diamond her fiance gave her. The romantic love affair between them was found out by Cal, Rose's fiance and Cal locked Jack out of jealousy. Soon afterwards, the ship hit an iceberg and began to sink. Jack and Rose must fight the death situation of the freezing water and await a rescue ship. The climax comes when Jack told Rose that the boat would be back soon and Rose watched him while saying I love you.

Let's move on to tell you why I like this movie. In my eyes, *TITANIC* is the most elaborate disaster movie ever made. It boasts the most amazing effects that I have ever seen up to now. To see a ship fall apart, with people running across the ship, flying across the deck, and falling to the water, is just amazing to look at. The effects are so stunningly realistic that you would swear you were looking at actual footage. To sum up, *TITANIC* is a romance, an adventure, and a thriller all rolled into one. It contains moments of exuberance, humor, pathos, and tragedy. In their own way, the characters are all larger-than-life, but they're human enough to capture our sympathy. Perhaps the most amazing thing about *TITANIC* is that, even though Cameron carefully recreates the death of the ship in all of its terrible grandeur, the event never eclipses the protagonists. To the end, we never cease caring about Rose and Jack.

Thank you for listening. I would like to hear your feelings about this movie and answer questions.

Case Study

If you were the CEO of an international company, how can you present the introduction to your company to your prospective business partner/your subordinates?

Useful Expressions

Word Bank:

image	without further ado	The floor is yours.
on behalf of	be in charge of	stay on schedule
competitive edge	take sb. from the roots of	mission statement
company philosophy		multilayered strategies
integrated skills	philosophy	outline
campaigns	overview	portfolio

Models for Reference

Practice with the expressions you have learned in this unit and refer to the Model Dialogue if necessary.

Model Dialogue 1

Bennett: Good morning, everyone. As you all know, we're searching for a suitable partner to help us undergo a change of image. It's my pleasure to welcome all of our guest speakers here today to The Flying Sharks. Our first presentation will be given by Pedro Hernandez. Mr. Hernandez is going to present his company Visual V Media. Without further ado, Mr. Hernandez, the floor is yours.

Hernandez: Thank you, Ms. Bennett. Good morning, everyone. On behalf of Visual V Media, I'd like to thank The Flying Sharks for inviting me here today. My name is Pedro Hernandez. I'm in charge of key accounts for the East Coast. I hope that by the end of my talk, I'll have convinced you of the value of a future business relationship with our company. Okay, if we're to stay on schedule, I should get started. I believe you'll find the next 30 minutes very interesting and informative. Today, I'll give you a clear picture of Visual V Media. I've organized my presentation into three main parts: the company background, our competitive edge

NOTES

and our current and future business projects. The first part, our company background, will take us from the roots of Visual V Media, to its size and its branches. And finally, we'll conclude the first section with a closer look at the Visual V Media's mission statement and company philosophy. Then, I'll move on to Part 2, our competitive edge. Here, I'll discuss our multilayered strategies and I'll present our integrated skills philosophy. To sum up, I'll provide you with a succinct outline of some of the campaigns we've designed, from the traditional ones to the more innovative. Finally, our third point, current and future business projects. Here, I'll start by giving you an overview of our portfolio, which will bring us to our current projects. And to conclude my talk, I'll discuss the three steps involved in our advertising campaign. As you can see, that's quite a lot to get through. Nevertheless, if you have questions, don't hesitate to interrupt. I'll be glad to try to answer them as we go along. Are you all with me? So, let's get started with the history of Visual V Media.

Model Dialogue 2

John: Good afternoon everyone. I'm pretty sure you have got the handouts at your hand. Mr. Smith from the Imperial Consultancy will outline the new solution for us.

Smith: Thank you Mr. John. Good afternoon everyone.

Sean: I will limit myself to the question to our possible solution for the problem we mentioned this morning. Please feel free to interrupt me if you have questions. The fact of the matter is that, a decade ago, 8 percent for R&D was sufficient. However, nowadays the market is a lot more demanding and the technology is constantly changing. I think you'll all agree that 8 percent no longer allows us to keep ahead in terms of technology. More detailed studies show that we're allocating too much of our budget to production. Let's go deeper and take a closer look at the root of the problem. I'd like to refer you to Page 3 of the handout. As is depicted by the chart, the amount of finance devoted to production is simply too high. Why is that? We looked into it and the real problem is that our means of production are too old, about 20 years. The machinery on our production line is outdated. I've prepared a few projections. Let me know if you can't see the screen. I'd like to draw your attention to this line chart. The blue line represents the initial investment needed for new machinery and the running costs for the next 10 years. The red one illustrates the estimated costs we will incur if we continue to use the machinery we've got. As the blue line indicates, the initial cost is substantial. However, with the new machinery, the breakeven point is reached after only five years.

In brief, we need to spend more to update our machinery in the budget.

Class Time for Topic-related Discussion

Suppose you are the project manager for a local communications company which provides internet services in Vietnam. Analyze the information below and prepare a two-minute presentation on the possibility of investing in this project.

Internet use in Vietnam

Location:	South East Asia
Population 2015:	90,500,000
Population breakdown by age:	Under 15 33%
	15-64 62%
	64+ 5%
Population growth 2008-2058:	96.31%
Internet uses 2003:	7,500
Internet uses 2012:	31,000,000
Growth in internet use 2000-2006:	6,460%
Total population using the internet:	34%

Further Reading

How to give an attractive presentation

To deliver an attractive presentation or speech, try first to find a topic to a focus that is suitable for your intended audience, because the over-basic topic will bore your audience. Then create an outline of your presentation which includes an introduction, a body and a conclusion.

In the introduction, welcome your audience, then introduce your subject, and purpose of your presentation. If this part is well delivered, you will be relaxed and confident in the "real" presentation of the body part.

In the body, which is the "real" part of your presentation, it should be well structured, divided up logically, with plenty of carefully spaced visuals. You can develop a set of bullet points that map out what you're going to say in each section. Focus on remembering the transitions from one bullet point to the next, and create some visual aids to attract the attention of your audience, such as PowerPoint slides, charts and images to accompany your speech. When using PowerPoint, keep it simple and do not repeat out words that are on the slide.

Finally, briefly restate each of the key points in your conclusion.

There are also some tips to make your presentations more attractive.

First, practice your presentations. It's just a matter of rehearsing enough times that the flow of words becomes natural.

Second, pay attention to your physical act on stage. For example, avoid repetitious hand gestures and phrases. When standing to give presentation, it's better to stand still and rely on hand gestures for emphasis. With a small audience, consider answering questions throughout the speech rather than in a question-and-answer period afterward.

Besides, dress professionally for your presentation. Keep a bottle of water handy. When you are too nervous to keep speech going on, take some water to relieve your nervousness and your audience won't sense it.

Things not to Miss

1. Background information
Making charts and figures in presentation

A picture is worth a thousand words. This is certainly true when you're presenting and explaining data. The trouble is there are so many different types of charts and graphs that it's difficult to know which one to choose. The following are four very common graph types:

Line graph They are most useful for showing trends, and for identifying whether two variables relate to (or "correlate with") one another.

Bar graph The higher or longer the bar is, the greater the value is.

Pie chart A pie chart compares parts to a whole. Be careful not to use too many segments in your pie chart. More than about six and it gets far too crowded.

Venn diagram This is a diagram used to show overlaps between sets of data.

NOTES

Once you have done your analyses and decided how to best present each one, think about how you will arrange them. There are many chart and diagram formats you can choose from when representing information graphically. Selecting the right type starts with a good understanding of how each is created.

2. Conversational skills

Speak in an interesting way in formal conversations

In any conversation, especially in formal ones, like presentation, your tone plays an important role in shortening the distance with the listener. Some speakers may want to come across as authoritative or wise or powerful or passionate, but it's usually much better to just sound conversational. Don't force it. Don't orate. Just be you.

In addition, eye contact is also incredibly powerful in conversation in talking. In formal conversations, say, speech or presentation, giving eye contact to your audience is a symbol of your confidence, which works well in having interaction with your audience. It's easy; you just need to find five or six friendly-looking people in different parts of the audience and look them in the eye as you speak. Think of them as friends you haven't seen in a year. It will do more than anything else to make your talk successful.

Unit 9   Talking about Trends

Five-minute Activity

In the description of performance, what are the elements that should be reckoned with? With these elements in mind, try to describe the sales of a product.

Useful Expressions

Word Bank : Market movements			
Upward movement	**Downward movement**	**Stability**	**Degree of change**
Climb	Decline	Flatten out	Slow
Rise	Decrease	Hold steady	Steady
Reach a high of	Drop	Level off	Slightly
Surge	Fall	Stabilize	Sharp
Rocket	Slide	Bounce back	Gradual
Roar	Crash	Stand at	Heavy
Gain	Collapse	Fluctuate	Massively
Jump	Plummet		Drastically
Rally	Take a fall		Dramatic
Strengthen	Weaken		Rapid
Recover /Pick up	Sink		Considerably
Shoot up	Reach a low of		
Reach a peak			

Models for Reference

Performance Description 1

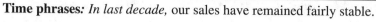

Time phrases*: In last decade,* our sales have remained fairly stable.

Verbs: During the first quarter, our direct costs *have risen.*

Nouns: This *drop* has put pressure on our margins.

Prepositions: In response we have cut retail price up to about 20%.

Qualifiers: There has also been a *sharp* fall in sales.

Cause and result: *As a result*, our margins have actually improved.

Performance Description 2

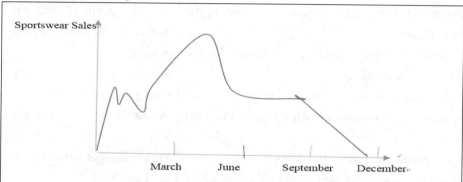

Sales have fluctuated in the first quarter. It grew rapidly in the following quarter and reached a peak. In the third quarter, it flattened off. And since then, it has dropped sharply.

Performance Description 3

It's been a roller coaster of a year with car sales fluctuating unpredictably. After a poor start in the first quarter, sales recovered in April and hit a peak in May, which is very early, compared to other years. It was probably due to the unusually hot weather. Anyway, as a result, production had to go into overdrive to get the products out. During the next four months, things stabilized and in October, when we normally do very well, sales actually dropped slightly. At that point, we decided to clear out our stock and started offering discount in the retail price of cars by 30%. The strategy worked amazingly well and led to a dramatic increase in sales, even though our margins fell.

Case Study

You are going to present the trend of the sales of a product. Note down possible reasons for the development in the graph, and give your presentation describing the development and the reasons.

Useful Expressions

Up & down market	Prediction
By the end of October, we witnessed a growth in the volume of trade.	Analysts predicted that the market would reach its peak in June.
This growth of about 6 percent was steady for the following 4 four months.	We expect to see a rise during the first quarter.
There have been no signs of a upward trend.	We anticipate some changes soon.
Some would say that we are witnessing a marginal decline.	We predict a drop in sales on the East Coast.
The sales figure dropped sharply last year.	We foresee some problems.
I thought that sales improved a little. No, I'm afraid that sales plummeted slightly.	We're awaiting the results of the investment.
The figures shoot up suddenly on the East Coast.	We think the management is likely of a change.
In April, it slumped to $36 because of Asian Crisis.	
Product stays at 300,000 in June. It increases to 550,000 in July. Then it fell back to 450, 000.	
Really? I thought we increased our market share substantially on the East Coast. Not at all. Our market share reached an all-time low on the East Coast.	

Models for Reference

Practice with the expressions you have learned in this unit and refer to the Model Dialogue if necessary.

Model Dialogue 1

Daniel: Ok, Phil, let's go over last year's sales figures.

Phil: Well, as you can see from the graph, during the first quarter, the running shoe sales stayed stable at 400,000 units per month.

Daniel: And then the Asian branch opened, right?

Phil: That's right. And you can see the sales went up to 500,000 unit in April, and then rose by another 100,000 in May and reached a peak of 600,000.

Daniel: Why was there a fall in July?

Phil: Well, that's mainly because our competitor has launched the new product.

Daniel: When did the recovery start?

Phil: Sales began to pick up in August and bounce back to 600,000 in the next two months.

Daniel: Why do you think there was such a growth?

Phil: Maybe the new product mania doesn't last long.

Daniel: It reached another peak of 800,000 in December.

Phil: It is quite reasonable. The sales jumped in the month due to Christmas holidays.

Daniel: So we finished much better than we started.

Phil: Yes, we did!

Model Dialogue 2

Kevin: Is everybody here? Good. Richard is going to go over last year's sportswear market in San Jose.

Richard: Thanks, Kevin. As you can see from the graph, the sales of sports equipment stayed stable at $30,000 in the first two months. However, after the market peaked at $32,000 in March, this trend started to reverse. We witnessed a downward trend in April and the situation stabilized in May and June when things leveled out, but this didn't last very long. Over the following quarter, that is, until September, the sales of sports equipment slumps. And it's still falling.

Kevin: Why do you think there was such a drop?

Richard: There has been an economic slowdown in the whole region. This downward trend has, of course, also affected buying power.

Fred: Is there any sign of a recovery?

Richard: Analysts are not expecting this trend to change anytime soon. As we can see here, they're even predicting a more substantial decline. According to the latest figures gathered by our market research department, the average household spent

NOTES

about $400 on sports equipment last year. This is quite a drop, approximately 20 percent down on the previous year, the lowest sales figure ever.

Fred: But the last two months results indicated a steady growth in the sales of sports equipment in that area.

Richard: That's easy—that's mainly because of the rush for Christmas.

Kevin: Well, if not downright falling, there still seems to be no sign of an immediate recovery in this year.

Richard: Yes. So, looking at these figures, we should probably consider our plans to close the shop in San Jose.

Class Time for Topic-related Discussion

Speculations give rise to severe and lasting economic crises such as The Wall Street Crash, the Tulipomania and the South Sea Bubble. Discuss with your partner about the following speculations. Present the trend of the following commodities and give your reasons. What will people speculate in during the next decade?

- gold
- precious stones
- property
- financial product

- currencies
- stocks and shares
- land/real estate
- insurance policy

- antique and paintings
- a young company or star-ups
- a high-interest deposit account
- a high-interest loan

Practice these key sentences.

- The prices will be pushed higher.
- Don't get caught up in this shady business.
- Figures show that sales of financial product were good/ sales plummeted. /The volume of trade increased drastically.
- The country has now suffers from investments./ has resolved to invest in grease./ increased its revenue.
- We expect to see a rise during the first quarter.
- Projections for the same period look better in Asia.

Further Reading

A global view of operations

Production is the creation of goods and services. Operations management is the set of activities that creates value in the form of goods and services by transforming inputs into outputs. Operations management is an area of management concerned with overseeing, designing, controlling the process of production and redesigning business operations in the production of goods and/or services. It involves the responsibility of ensuring that business operations are efficient in terms of using as few resources as needed, and effective in terms of meeting customer requirements. It is concerned with managing the process that converts inputs (in the forms of materials, labor, and energy) into outputs (in the form of goods and/or services).

In organizations that do not create physical products the production function may be less obvious. It may be "hidden" from the public and even from the customer. Examples are the transformations that take place at a bank, hospital, airline office, or college.

Often when services are performed, no tangible goods are produced. Instead, the product may take such forms as the transfer of funds from a saving account to a checking account, the transplant of a liver, the filling of an empty seat on an airline, or the education of a student. Regardless of whether the end product is a good or service, the production activities that go on in the organization are often referred to as operations or operations management.

There are many reasons why a domestic business operation will decide to change to some form of international operation. These can be viewed as a continuum ranging from tangible reasons to intangible reasons.

Things not to Miss

1. Background information

Inside sales vs. Outside sales Since the advent of the telephone, a distinction has been made between "inside sales" and "outside sales" although it is generally agreed that those terms have no hard-and-fast definition. In the United States, the Fair Labor Standards Act defines outside sales representatives as "employees (who) sell their employer's products, services, or facilities to customers away from their employer's place(s) of business, in general, either at the customer's place of business or by selling door-to-door at the customer's home" while defining those who work "from the employer's location" as inside sales. Inside sales generally involves attempting to close business primarily over the phone via telemarketing, while outside sales (or "field" sales) will usually involve initial phone work to book sales calls at the potential buyer's location to attempt to close the deal in person. Some companies have an inside sales department that works with outside representatives and book their appointments for them. Inside sales sometimes refers to upselling to existing customers.

The relationships between sales and marketing Marketing and sales differ greatly, but have the same goal. Selling is the final stage in Marketing, which also includes Pricing, Promotion, Place and Product (the 4 Ps). A marketing department in an organization has the goals of increasing the desirability and value to the customer and increasing the number and engagement of interactions between potential customers and the organization. Achieving this goal may involve the sales team using promotional techniques such as advertising, sales promotion, publicity, and public relations, creating new sales channels, or creating new products (new product development), among other things. It can also include bringing the potential customer to visit the organization's website(s) for more information, or to contact the organization for more information, or to interact with the organization via social media such as Twitter, Facebook and blogs.

2. Conversational skills

Improving negotiation skills

1) Learn to flinch

A flinch is a visible reaction to an offer or price. The objective of this negotiation strategy is to make the other people feel uncomfortable about the offer they presented. When you quote a price for a specific product, flinching means you respond by exclaiming, "You want how much?!" You must appear shocked and surprised that they could be bold enough to request that figure. Unless the other person is a well-seasoned negotiator, they will respond in one of two ways: a) they will become very uncomfortable and begin to try to rationalize their price; b) they will offer an immediate concession.

2) Recognize that people often ask for more than they expect to get

You need to resist the temptation to automatically reduce your price or offer a discount. When asked for a hefty discount, usually you are not expected agreeing to the request.

3) Do your homework

You need to learn as much about the other person's situation. Ask more questions about their purchase. Learn what is important to them as well as their needs and wants. It is also important to learn as much about your competitors as possible. This will help you defeat possible price objections and prevent someone from using your competitors as leverage.

4) Maintain your walk away power

It is better to walk away from a sale rather than make too large a concession or give a deep discount of your product or service. This negotiation strategy gives the most leverage when dealing with other well-reasoned negotiators.

Unit 10   Making Decisions and Summing up

Five-minute Activity

Do you like to keep your options open or do you prefer to decide on something quickly? Sum up all the important decisions you have made in the past five years and explain why.

Useful Expressions

Expressing for making decisions	Expressions for summaries
Stranding on the fence	Briefly/ in brief
To change my mind	Altogether
To have second thoughts	In the final/ last analysis
To make up my mind	The long and the short of it
To give it a lot of thought	On balance
to be in two minds about something	To the effect that
To make a tentative decision	In one word
We weigh up his options.	I draw the conclusion that…
We keep your options open.	

Sentences for making decision

Do you give things a lot of thought before making a decision?

Have you ever made a big decision and then changed your mind?

Are you good at weighing up your options before deciding on fomenting?

Do you like to keep your options open or do you prefer to decide on something quickly?

Models for Reference

Fred: We need to come to an agreement on this. Rossi, what do you think?

Rossi: I think we should consider Bob Walton to do this design.

Fred: What's your opinion, Tara?

Tara: I'm quite open to all those mentioned.

Fred: We have to take action on this. Who would you recommend, Mary?

Mary: Barnes Co. seems to be more suitable.

Tara: Mary is right. I'd recommend Barnes Co..

Fred: Hmm ... Let's see a show of hands. Those of you in favor of Bob Walton, please raise your hands. Good. And who's in support of Barnes Co.? I believe the result is clear. Six to two in favor of Barnes Co.!

Tara: Now that we've reached a consensus, I'll get in touch with the agent of Barnes Co.

Fred: Good. So, we've come to the end of the agenda. I know we're all tired, but before we close, I think we should go over the main points again.

All: Absolutely.

Case Study

How can you sum up a report?

Useful Expressions

Word Bank :

take action	crossover appeal	in favor of
reach a consensus	agent	go over
sum up	contract	reach a decision
input	look into	call it a day

Models for Reference

Practice with the expressions you have learned in this unit and refer to the Model Dialogue if necessary.

Model Dialogue 1

Smith: So to sum up, correct me if I'm wrong, Steve. Item 1 was Mary's presentation.

Excellent work, I think we all agree. We decided for Item 2 that Ruth would start looking for a new advertising partner.

Steve: And if I may add, we also agreed that they would cancel our current contract with Bob Walton.

Smith: Thank you, Steve. We couldn't reach a decision on Items 3 and 4 because Mark's opinions are needed. Mary will arrange another meeting. Can you confirm with him ASAP?

Steve: Definitely.

Smith: Item 5: Colin will look into the technology required and report to the board by the end of next week. As for the image problem, Tara is going to contact the agent of Barnes Co. Have I forgotten anything, Steve?

Steve: No, that covers everything.

Smith: Okay. Finally, Steve will send a copy of today's minutes to all present. Mary, did you want to add anything?

Mary: No, I believe that's everything.

Smith: Good. Well, that sums it all up. Before we call it a day, I'd like to thank you all again for taking part today. I only regret that we're finished so soon. That means I'll have to take you all out to dinner tonight.

All: Ah!

Model Dialogue 2

Jane : Now we all agree that the company is making a loss. What we've got to do now is to cut the costs. Mitchell, can you bring us up to date?

Mitchell: Yes. Well we have all agreed that we should make 50 employees redundant and pay no end-of-year bonuses. But we are still not sure whether we must reduce everyone' salary by 6%. Monica, is there anything to add?

Monica: And if I may add, the alternative way to solve the problem may be to cut factory workers' wages by 8%.

Jane: Well, we need more information about where we're going. So the next thing to do is to strike a balance between wage cutting and the workers' devotion. Later, Steve will send a copy of today's minutes to all present. Thank you for your time.

Class Time for Topic-related Discussion

Your company is to hold an entertaining party for all staff. Some think it should be held on weekend, while others prefer to have it on an evening on work days. Arrange a discussion and then ask representatives from both parties to summarize key points.

Practice these key sentences.

- I am having second thoughts about …
- Thank you for your views, I will take them into consideration.
- It is difficult to make up my mind about the right choice.
- I'm in two minds about what to do.
- I made a rash decision.
- I just want to keep my options open for now.
- Before we close, let me summarize the main points.

Further Reading

Summarizing and concluding a discussion

Without a good conclusion, no discussion is really complete. One way to finish a discussion is to summarize briefly the main arguments and draw conclusions for the audience. It is extremely important that you do not simply finish your talk but rather spend some time recapping the main points. Everyone involved in the discussion needs to be accurately informed of the concluded information. Summarize correctly and accurately will be a factor in the meeting's ultimate success.

Referring back Summarize the discussion of the meeting in a brief statement. The objective of this part is to ensure the participants to get a clear idea of what we have discussed in the meeting.

As we mentioned earlier in the discussion, the focus of this meeting is to discuss how the work process transition directly affects your position in the human resource department.

As we were saying a few minutes ago, there are many pitfalls and dangers in takeovers and mergers that you really have to consider carefully.

Summarizing the agreement reached and disagreement left behind This part aims to keep the participants informed of the decision made and the issues need to be discussed in the future meeting.

As we can see from the discussion, we have reached an agreement on the work needs to be done in the sphere of sales and marketing. And we also agreed that we can't rely on Target Store's support much longer. We still can't reach a decision on the contract with Marion Haynes since Tim Reid is absent.

Asking for feedback To err is human. More often than not, you will miss something in your summary. To perfect the summary, we can try to get the relative response from the participants and be sure they get informed of the decision.

Is there any area I haven't covered?

What's missing?

Planning for future Thank the employees for the time that they take out of their work schedule to attend the meeting. Also, state something along the lines of how to carry out the decision made in the meeting. This last bit of information is just a common courtesy. It also helps the employees to be more prepared for the following mission.

Things not to Miss

1. Background information

Marion Haynes Marion Haynes is a famous writer who enjoys a great reputation in how to make decisions for a more productive meeting. Eight steps for decision-making are recommended as follows:

1) Discuss and make an analysis of the situation.
2) Define what the problem is.
3) Set an objective.
4) Present what is essential and desirable.
5) Think of alternatives.
6) Work out how to evaluate the alternatives.
7) Evaluate them.
8) Choose among them.

2. Conversational skills

Be more flexible

During the discussion or negotiation, more often than not agreement is not available. In order to ensure that the agenda can go smoothly, we have to be more flexible. "I think we should leave this point and come back to it later." Here come the cases:

Yang: I'm afraid we can't. This is the best price we can quote.

Amanda: **Let's leave that for the time being.**

Amanda: Your price is higher than I can accept. Could you come down a little?

Yang: **What would you suggest?**

Amanda: Could you make it 40 pence per yard, CIF London?

"Can we just summarize the points we've agreed so far?" After they have reached agreement on most issues, it is more likely that both parties would like to make some compromise to close the deal.

Unit 11　The Company

Five-minute Activity

Your company is launching a new product. Discuss about what information your company needs to decide on to launch its new product.

Useful Expressions

Word Bank : New Product

HP printer	Lenovo laptop	Crest Toothpaste
Kiehl's face wash	Bianca shampoo	LG TV set
Schiff Move Free	Porsche	Maserati
Nike Airmax	Gree Microwave Oven	Midea rice cooker
Samsung home movie system		Vitafusion Gummy Vites Vitamin
Basle Ear-hook Coffee	Nutrilite calcium magnesium	

Models for Reference

Presenting a Product 1

Name: Hairglow

Selling prices: $15 & $28

Bottle sizes: 300ml & 500ml

Target markets: Women who buy the product for themselves or the family

Age group: 18-35 & 50 +

Income groups: Middle & High

Main outlets: Supermarkets, Hairdressers, Pharmacies & Exclusive shops

Presenting a Product 2

Name: Supor Rice Cooker

Model: CFXB40FC8155

Colors: black, grey, golden & red

Sizes: for 4-6 family members

Feature: computer-controlled, smart design, easy to operate

Selling prices: $116

Target markets: Women who buy the product for the family

Age group: 25-35 & 50 +

Income groups: Middle & High

Main outlets: Supermarkets, Shopping Mall & Exclusive shops

Delivery: within 3 days

Case Study

Show your partner around your company, talk about the different departments of the company and describe what is happening now.

Useful Expressions

- New premises have been bought in Texas.
- The customer service department is not on this floor.
- Hi, Lydia, welcome to the Inditex group.
- OK, well, let me show you around. Straight ahead here you'll see the R&D department.
- Here's the purchasing department. Alice Baumann was promoted to the purchasing manager last year.
- The HR is on the second floor. That's Carlos there. He's head of Human Resources.
- As you can see, here we have the sales and marketing department. Mr. Dell is the head of it. And John is an intern in the sales department.
- Now on our right here is the PR department, and next to it is the customer service department.
- OK, well, that's pretty much everything on this floor.
- Upstairs are the most important place, the executive offices and the main conference

rooms.

■ And downstairs is the Shipping department, R&D and the IT department.

Models for Reference

Practice with the expressions you have learned in this unit and refer to the Model Dialogue if necessary.

Model Dialogue 1

Lydia: Hi, Cristina, welcome to the Citi Bank.

Cristina: Thanks, Lydia. It's great to be here. I am a bit nervous now. You know, first day and all.

Lydia: Oh, I quite understand. But you don't have to worry. We have interns studying here all the time. Ok, well, then let me show you around. Straight ahead here is the Main Hall, where we serve customers. As you can see, Bill is talking to a customer. He is a well-respected cashier.

Cristina: OK.

Lydia: Now, on our left here is the Reception desk. The staff here answer questions and complaint from customers.

Cristina: Ah... So I'll be working in there, will I?

Lydia: Yeah, you will work with Sandra and Maggie. I'll take you there once I've shown you everything.

Cristina: Sounds good.

Lydia: Now, on our right, here we have the Currency section. Customers can exchange foreign currency here. That's Peter there. He's head of this section.

Cristina: Right.

Lydia: OK, well, that's pretty much everything on this floor. Upstairs you'll find the manager's office. And next to it is the Loans section, which assists Mr. Benetti, our manager to arrange loans for customers. By the way, Mr. Benetti wants to talk to you and you can drop by his office later.

Cristina: OK.

Lydia: And finally, downstairs is the most important place, the place you'll find out everything you need to know—the canteen.

Cristina: Ah...Of course. Thank you for showing me around.

Lydia: My pleasure.

Model Dialogue 2

Mary: Hello, Welcome to Hillcrest Hotel.

Michael: Mary Clarence! Hi, Mary, long time no see.

Mary: Hi, and you are…?

Michael: Oh, I'm Michael Warren. We are high school classmates, remember?

Mary: Yeah, I do remember, but you are quite normal!

Michael: Well, I know what you mean. I'm a lawyer now. So you work here?

Mary: Yeah, I work as a receptionist here, welcoming guests, answering calls, talking to guest, etc.

Michael: Could you show me to the bedroom?

Mary: Of course. But now, the maid is cleaning the room, and maybe I can show you around.

Michael: That's great!

Mary: Straight ahead here is the restaurant. We serve breakfast, lunch and dinner. The waiters are cleaning tables.

Michael: OK.

Mary: Here on our left is the kitchen. At the moment the chefs are preparing today's meal.

Michael: Right.

Mary: As you can see, here we have the gift shop where you can buy some souvenirs for your family members and friends. Monica is a talented sales assistant and she will help you to choose the gifts.

Michael: Sounds great!

Mary: OK, well, that's pretty much everything on this floor. Upstairs are the Hotel Reservation Department. We can check in there.

Michael: Thanks!

Mary: My pleasure!

Class Time for Topic-related Discussion

Think of a product and use four or five expressions (verb+preposition) to describe

NOTES

it. See if your partner can guess what the product is from the statements.

Practice these key sentences.
- It consists of four main parts.
- It retails at $20.
- Well, the first prototype was marketed in July of 2014.
- It complies with industry standards.
- It will appeal to students.
- Only a few months before, the product was launched.
- It is designed to withstand high temperatures.
- It comes in two different sizes.
- We employed shock absorption to develop the product.
- It is sold mainly in hardware stores.

Example: They retail at about $40. They come in range of sizes and colors. They are aimed at the youth market mainly, although some older people wear them too. They are sold in sports shops. They are designed to be light and comfortable. (Answer: training shoes)

Further Reading

Strategic Management

The increasing importance of strategic management may stem from several trends. Increasing competition in most industries has made it difficult for some companies to compete. Modern and cheaper transportation and communication have led to increasing global trade. Technological development has caused accelerated changes in the global economy.

Strategic management is an approach to identifying and making the necessary changes and measuring the organization's performance as it moves toward its vision.

It is the responsibility of senior leadership to strategically manage the organization. Strategic management is a continuous process rather than a one-time event. Therefore, the senior leaders need to be strategic thinkers and leaders of the organization and its culture, changing it as necessary.

To be the most successful, leaders must become facilitators, coaches, consultants, and consensus-builders. Transformational leadership is described by Bernard Bass as, superior leadership performance that occurs when leaders broaden and elevate the interests of their employees, when they generate awareness and acceptance of the purposes and mission of the group, and when they stir their employees to look beyond their own self-interest for the good of the group. Acquiring transformational leadership traits requires hard work and dedication, willingness to take some risks, and internalizing the organization's vision and guiding principles.

Strategic management consists of five processes: pre-planning, strategic planning, deployment, implementation, and measurement and evaluation. The first three components together give direction to the enterprise, establish the blue map for strategic action, and, in effect, define the organization's strategic plan. The fourth component is the most complicated and challenging one because it involves both deciding on and undertaking the administrative actions needed to convert the strategic plan into results; indeed, the successful execution of strategy takes probably 5 to 10 times more time-consuming than formulating the strategic plan. The fifth component, evaluating strategic performance and making corrective adjustments, is not only the end but also the beginning of the strategic management cycle. The match of external and internal events guarantees that the time will come for making revisions in the four previous components. Most of the time, revisions will be of the fine-tuning variety, but occasions for major overhaul in one or more components arise—sometimes because of significant external developments and sometimes because of sharply sliding financial performance.

Things not to Miss

1. Background information

Research and development (R&D), also known in Europe as research and technical (or technological) development (RTD), is a general term for activities in connection with corporate or governmental innovation. The activities that are classified as R&D differ from company to company, but there are two primary models, with an R&D department being either staffed by engineers and tasked with directly developing new products, or staffed with industrial scientists and tasked with applied research in scientific or technological fields which may facilitate future product development. In either case, R&D differs from the vast majority of corporate activities in that it is not often intended to yield immediate profit, and generally carries greater risk and an uncertain return on investment.

Public relations (PR) is the practice of managing the spread of information between an individual or an organization (such as a business, government agency, or a nonprofit organization) and the public. Public relations may include an organization or individual gaining exposure to their audiences using topics of public interest and news items that do not require direct payment. This differentiates it from advertising as a form of marketing communications. The aim of public relations is to inform the public, prospective customers, investors, partners, employees, and other stakeholders and ultimately persuade them to maintain a certain view about the organization, its leadership, products, or of political decisions. Public relations professionals typically work for PR and marketing firms, businesses and companies, government, government agencies, and public officials as PIOs, and nongovernmental organizations and nonprofit organizations.

2. Conversational skills
What to talk over lunch with colleagues?

There are so many things to talk about. You just need to pick up a common ground that is interesting for both of you. Do not try to impress anyone by just trying to talk artificially for the sake of benefit. You should have the passion to build a good relationship not just for work but also for making good friends.

It is very important you find some common ground to have a friendly conversation that is not related to work. Typically people in US follow lot of sports. Depending on the time of year, most of them follow some sports. It can be American football(NFL), basketball(NBA), world series baseball, college football, ice hockey or any other local sport. A good conversation would be discussing about a game that happened last night. If you do not know the game, it is hard. You probably have to learn the rules and maybe follow for a little bit to be able to have a good conversation. Again, you are not trying to impress someone artificially for the sake of benefit. You just have to have the passion for sports and do it naturally. If your colleagues have kids, they may coach their kids or someone. You can talk about the sports they coach or how the game went. People do not talk about family directly, because it is very personal and no one shares with colleagues unless they know you well. You do not want to enter someone's personal space directly. So, do not just jump into personal stuff. Just try to talk about something the other person is passionate about and you also like. Also, you can talk about movies that were released last week and see what's good and not. You may talk about social or economic issues. You can talk about cultural topics. Ask about American culture and know they will be happy to explain on the same direction, and you have to share as they ask. You can talk about politics, but you have to be very careful, it can create differences of opinion if you do not know what belief the person holds to. Avoid any debating subjects. It can be good or may be totally bad for you. People talk about weather a lot in America. Talk about anything that was a news event in recent times. Talk about stock market.

Unit 12   Company Resources

□□□□□□□□ ➪

Five-minute Activity

Human capital occupies a rather prominent position in the company resources. You are supposed to conduct a survey about the human capital in different companies, including people's working conditions, salary & income, position, types of employment, etc.

Useful Expressions

Word Bank: Human capital

Employment	Salary & income	Working time	Hiring & firing
Wage earner Personal assistant Staff Manager Employer Employee Freelancer Trainee Part-timer Full-timer	Income/ Pay /Salary Earnings Living wage Low /Hourly wage Incentive wage Earned income Remuneration Performance-related Pay Raise Bonus Perk	Flexitime Overtime Full-time Part-time Day shift Graveyard shift Double shift	Hire Employ Recruit Let go of Lay off Dismiss Sack Fire Overstaff Understaff Adequately staff

Models for Reference

Human Capital 1

I work at a local real estate company, the only wage earner in our house. Most of the employees like working for the Vedanta Designs. There are a couple of hundred but not more than 500 on the payroll, including part-timers, freelancers and trainees. Definitely, it's understaffed. Employees are not allowed to jobshare in our company. If I'm on a scale from one to ten with one being very poor and ten being excellent, I would rate myself 7.

Human Capital 2

I used to do the full time 40-hour-week thing for 10 years, meeting a lot of new people and assisting wherever necessary. I have a lot of responsibilities, so my salary is high, too. But I hated it. I felt as if I was chained to the company. Once the kids get a little older and I am not the only one bringing money into the home, I have options to work on different projects for different companies. A lower salary as I gain, at least that's my decision. And of course the best part is that I send a bill to the project manager telling him exactly how many hours I worked. I would rate my working conditions 9 on the scale from one to ten with one being very poor and ten excellent.

Case Study

The SWOT (strengths, weaknesses, opportunities, threats) analysis serves as the dominant factor for the corporate strategy making. Make an SWOT analysis of the company, service or product available, identify its strengths, weaknesses, opportunities & threats, and provide your recommendations.

Useful Expressions

Strengths

What are your organization's core strengths?

What unique resources are available?

What strengths can be acquired?

Core/ Distinctive competencies in vehicle production

A strong financial condition, ample financial resources to grow the business

Product innovation capabilities/wide geographic coverage/strong advertising and promotion/superior intellectual capital/better product quality/cost advantages

Weaknesses

What are the perceived weaknesses?

What resources are inadequate?

How will your company overcome the weaknesses?

What weaknesses can't be overcome?

A weak balance sheet, burdened with too much debt/lack of management

Too narrow a product line relative to rivals/losing market share

Behind rivals in e-commerce capabilities/too much underutilized plant capacity/ weak dealer networks/lack of global distribution capability

Opportunities

What is the value of the present opportunity?

Will the value be enhanced by the follow-up contracts?

Will your company's core strength be fit for achieving the value?

Sharply rising buyer demand for the product/utilizing the existing technological know-how to enter new product lines/ online sales/falling trade barriers in attractive foreign markets/exploit emerging new technology/entering into alliances to boost competitive capability

Threats

Are there any conditions that reduce the value?

What is the level of competition?

Will your weaknesses limit your success?

Increasing intensity of competition/restrictive policies on the part of the government/vulnerability to unfavorable industry driving forces/a shift in buyer needs and taste/loss of sales to substitute products

Models for Reference

Practice with the expressions you have learned in this unit and refer to the Model Dialogue if necessary.

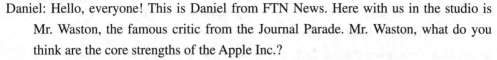

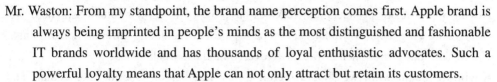

Model Dialogue 1

Daniel: Hello, everyone! This is Daniel from FTN News. Here with us in the studio is Mr. Waston, the famous critic from the Journal Parade. Mr. Waston, what do you think are the core strengths of the Apple Inc.?

Mr. Waston: From my standpoint, the brand name perception comes first. Apple brand is always being imprinted in people's minds as the most distinguished and fashionable IT brands worldwide and has thousands of loyal enthusiastic advocates. Such a powerful loyalty means that Apple can not only attract but retain its customers.

Daniel: That also provides Apple with opportunity to extend new products to the customers.

Mr. Waston: That's right. It cost far less to keep an existing customer than to lure in a new one. Meanwhile, Apple Inc.'s innovation keeps it a front-runner in electronics.

Daniel: Yeah, the R&D department always comes up with stylish design and user-friendly interfaces. However, every coin has two sides. What are the perceived weaknesses?

Mr. Waston: The high pricing ranks as the most vulnerability for the Apple Inc. compared with its rivals. What's more, the non-compatibility can obstruct some potential customers.

Daniel: So what strategy will it adopt in the next decade?

Mr. Waston: Presumably, it will lower the cost, enter into alliances or joint venture and focus on the core competence, its innovation to expand.

Daniel: Thanks for your remarkable comment.

Mr. Waston: My pleasure.

Model Dialogue 2

Colin: Hi, Kevin! The battle between us and 360 indeed challenges our monopoly status, which indicates that we are facing urgent crisis and competition. As the director of the board, what's your opinion?

Kevin: As I see it, we not only have to develop our core competence but also should focus on working on our weaknesses.

Colin: When you mention weaknesses, can you give us some specific examples?

Kevin: Yes. First priority should go to the cultivation of self-innovation ability. Many of our products and services are imitating from other companies. Therefore, some netizens even describe us as a follower rather than a leader. Without strong innovation ability, we have less advantage and will lose more market share in the process of globalization.

Colin: That's really impressive. Any other weaknesses that limit our growth?

Kevin: Some of our products and services have the quite similar functions. Therefore, we are even faced with internal competition for users among different departments.

Colin: Yes, that's true. Then how can we overcome these weaknesses?

Kevin: To begin with, we should recruit a vast number of superior intellectuals and develop more new products with our intellectual property rather than imitate other companies. Secondly, we should deepen the management and settle the internal conflicts in racing for users. Finally, chances are good that we can cooperate more with foreign companies and gain more market share both at home and abroad.

Colin: I agree.

Class Time for Topic-related Discussion

Suppose that you are the manager of a small private guard firm with 60 employees. Your company has been servicing 3 communities in the downtown area. You have recently heard that 2 large communities in the nearby block are looking for a new security service. It would be quite lucrative but you would have to double the size of your company to handle it. Make your SWOT analysis of the situation and endeavor to win the contract.

Practice these key sentences.

- Our firm has a distinctive competence in security surveillance.
- We have close relations with other security companies.
- We have contracted and cooperated with other private guard firms to meet the load before.
- We are not experienced in servicing large communities.
- We have inadequate manpower and limited time to enlarge the company.
- It will be very lucrative and there are more communities being constructed in that block.
- We must recruit additional guards due to the limited number of guards available.

Further Reading

Human resource management and competitive advantage

Human resource management

An organization's human resource management (HRM) function focuses on the human-centered aspect of management. It consists of practices that make it possible for the organization to deal effectively with its employees during the various phases of the employment cycle: pre-selection, selection, and post-selection.

Gaining a competitive advantage

Firms can gain a competitive advantage over competitors via effective management of their human resources. In this section we introduce the notion of competitive advantage and then discuss how firms can achieve and sustain it through effective HRM practices.

Competitive advantage and HRM

Competitive advantage occurs when an organization acquires or develops an attribute or combination of attributes that enables it to outperform its competitors.

The HRM practices of an organization can be an important source of competitive advantage. As we shall see, effective HRM practices can enhance a firm's competitive advantage by creating both cost leadership and product differentiation. This assertion will be documented with evidence derived from research and expert opinion in the following paragraphs.

Evidence linking HRM practices and competitive advantage

A growing body of research-based evidence indicates that a firm's HRM practices can have a rather strong impact on competitive advantage. One study is cited in the following part that examined the impact of the entire set of HRM practices used by various companies.

One study examined the HRM practices and productivity levels of 869 firms across 32 industries. The quality or sophistication of each company's set of HRM practices was rated based on the presence of such things as incentive plans, employee grievance systems, formal performance appraisal systems, and worker participation in decision making. The study unfolded a strong link between HRM sophistication ratings and productivity levels—company with high HRM ratings clearly outperformed those with

NOTES

low ones. Specifically, a difference of one standard deviation in HRM sophistication ratings translated to a productivity difference of five percent. Essentially, this finding means that a company rated well above average out-produced the "average" company by five percent.

Things not to Miss

1. Background information

Human capital is the stock of knowledge, habits, social and personality attributes, including creativity, embodied in the ability to perform labor so as to produce economic value. Alternatively, human capital is a collection of resources—all the knowledge, talents, skills, abilities, experience, intelligence, training, judgment, and wisdom possessed individually and collectively by individuals in a population. These resources are the total capacity of the people that represents a form of wealth which can be directed to accomplish the goals of the nation or state or a portion thereof.

2. Conversational skills
How to end a conversation politely

Even when a conversation is interesting, you sometimes have to end it before the other person is ready. It's also the case for business. In business, finding a polite way to break off a conversation is as tricky as it is critical. Time is money, so you don't want to chit-chat with a client or a colleague longer than necessary. Here are some ways to depart gracefully.

The first way is to use body language to sign that you want to end the conversation, such as a wandering gaze, a small step away from him/her, increasingly shorter responses to what he or she says, putting things in a bag or putting on a jacket or sweater.

Besides body language, you can also offer the reasons why you have to leave before saying bye. For instance, "Look at the time! I'm afraid I'll have another appointment. Bye from now. Take care."

Offering an apology is also a good choice. "I'm sorry but I have some things I have to get done today." Remaining polite but firm helps you exit the conversation gracefully.

Looking to the future can also save the embarrassment of your sudden departure. You can wait for a pause and offer a handshake and say, "It was great talking with you. See you later."

Unit 13   Help Wanted

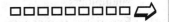

Five-minute Activity

Design a job advertisement for the company. Think about what should be included in it.

Useful Expressions

Benefits	Employment status
Work-life balance	I've got a part-time job.
Pay & benefits	I've got a full-time job.
Job security & advancement	I'm unemployed/ out of work/ looking for a job.
Management	I'm not working at the moment.
Salary	I've been made redundant.

Occupation

What do you do?

What do you do for a living?

What sort of work do you do?

What line of work are you in?

Models for Reference

Job Advertisement

Catchment Restoration Managers

We are seeking to employ several Catchment Restoration Managers. The primary purpose of the Managers will be to deliver on-ground flood recovery works such as erosion control, fencing, revegetation and weed management across the South Central region.

We are seeking individuals who have:

- knowledge of the principles and practices of environmental management
- experience in the planning, budgeting, timely implementation and review of on-ground works
- demonstrated commitment to safety and compliance
- the ability to work with a range of stakeholders including partner agencies and landholders
- Experience in managing contractors in the delivery of on-ground works

For further information, please refer to the position description at www.sccma.com. Alternatively contact the SCCMA on (03)5778 7677.

All Expressions of Interest are to be submitted by the close of business 17 March 2017 and should contain a resume plus cover letter addressing the key selection criteria within the position description. Please mail to hrmanager@sccma.com or post to the HR Manager, SCCMA, PO Box 39 Huntly VIC 4553.

Case Study

Can you describe reasons why you have chosen a career (position, company)?

Useful Expressions

international sales	enthusiastic	executives
self- starting	professional	track
corporation	qualification	graduate
fluency	mandatory	advantageous
salary	remuneration	package
CV	results-oriented	record

Models for Reference

Practice with the expressions you have learned in this unit and refer to the Model Dialogue if necessary.

NOTES

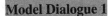

Model Dialogue 1

Terry: Hey. Here's an interesting job. This is just what I'm looking for. Telco, part of a large and diverse international group, is looking for international sales executives and I might be just right for the job.

Michael: International sales executives? Sounds interesting!

Terry: Well, they're looking for self-starting, enthusiastic and results-oriented professionals with a track record in international business development.

Michael: That sounds like you.

Terry: Yes. And they want experience in developing marketing materials as well as a background of selling products or services to large corporations and institutions.

Michael: Does it say what kind of qualifications they're looking for?

Terry: First of all, they want a graduate with four years' relevant experience. They're also looking for good computer skills. Fluency in English is mandatory and other languages, they say, would be advantageous.

Michael: That's you, more or less. Is there anything about the salary?

Terry: It says that there will be an attractive remuneration package.

Michael: OK. What are you waiting for? Get that CV in the mail right away.

Model Dialogue 2

Kevin: Welcome to Campbell Company.

Tony: I am glad for the chance to be interviewed.

Kelvin: Tell me about yourself.

Tony: Well as you can see from my resume, I've worked as an electrical engineer for 10 years now. Your company is large and there is plenty of room for advancement. So I think it is a good career move to join your company.

Kelvin: I see. Are you available to work overtime?

Tony: Yes, I like to work hard and I like to make money. That's also why I am applying for a job with your company.

Kelvin: You seem to be the kind of employee we are looking for. If we decide to hire you, when can you start?

Tony: Immediately.

Kelvin: OK, welcome aboard.

Tony: Great, thank you for your time. I look forward to working with you.

Class Time for Topic-related Discussion

Suppose you are the director of the HR Department. You and your colleagues are considering now about hiring new salespeople. Discuss with them of all qualities salespeople need and requirements for this job.

Practice these key sentences.

- Amanda has been working for 3 years.
- She is a good team-player.
- Warren has always set himself goals and it motivates him to work hard.
- What makes him fit for this company?
- Diana is always looking for new challenges.

Further Reading

Tips for searching job

Looking for a new job can become a job in itself; however, if you plan your search correctly, you could be on your way to a great new career sooner than you think.

Here's some advice on the key things you need to do to make your job hunt a resounding success.

Firstly, don't be a copycat candidate. Having copies of your resume and cover letter ready to edit is far from being enough. You can change the content to match the requirements of the job you're applying for and personalize cover letters for your own correspondence.

Secondly, review samples. It's always a good idea to look at sample letters and resumes to get ideas for your own job search materials.

Thirdly, use job search engines. Use the job search engine sites to search the major job boards, company sites, associations, and other sites with job postings for you. You will be able to search all the jobs posted online in one step.

Fourthly, use your network. Networking is getting to know people who can help you develop your career prospects. You can just tell everyone you know that you are looking for work and keep your ears open and listen for information that could work to your advantage.

Last, be realistic. Be honest about what you can realistically offer to a new employer. It's tempting to apply for a more challenging and prestigious role, but make sure you have both the skills and the commitment to be successful.

Taking into account these five tips will broaden your job search resources and can best position you for success in a competitive job market. Good luck!

Things not to Miss

1. Background information

The Wall Street Journal is an American English-language international daily newspaper with a special emphasis on business and economic news. Starting publication in 1889 and having a circulation of about 2.4 million copies (including nearly 900,000 digital subscriptions), it is the largest newspaper in the U.S. by circulation.

The Journal primarily covers U.S. economic and international business topics, and financial news and issues. Deriving its name from Wall Street located in New York City, which is the heart of the financial district, it has readers mostly from economic, financial, political, academic circles, medical field and stock market. Including 0.2 million executives and most managers in Top 500 Companies in the U.S. are its readers. The newspaper version has won the Pulitzer Prize thirty-four times, including 2007 prizes for its reporting on backdated stock options and the adverse effects of China's booming economy.

2. Conversational skills

Impress the interviewer. Leave the interviewer with the impression that you are the one who makes his job easier. The interviewer cares not how awesome you think the job is but what benefits you can bring to this job! So stop talking how appealing this job is! Review the job description and note down the job requirements. Focus on your achievements, education，skills and experience relevant to the job requirements and the company's needs. Refer to your previous successes and your goals for the future. Be straightforward and confident about your abilities and skills. The skills and abilities you mention must be relevant to the position and organization you are interviewing for.   For example, "I am the person for this job because I have the drive and motivation to do my very best every day". Or "what makes me suitable for this position is my commitment." Once I commit, I try my best to fulfill my commitment and make sure no staff gets a complaint against me. I possess good communication skills and have an eye for detail. I am hard-working, energetic and have the ability to take on challenges. A potential employer wants to know you are self-driven and self-motivated. They want to know that they will not have to look over your shoulder as you work or tell you what to do twice.

Unit 14   The Interview

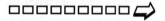

Five-minute Activity

How would you try to impress your interviewer when doing a job interview?

Useful Expressions

Describing your personality	Describing your strengths
Easy-going	The ability to multitask
Hard-working	Perform to a deadline
Committed	Solve problems
Trustworthy	Communicate well
Honest	Work in an international environment and with
Focused	people from all over the world
Methodical	Enthusiasm
Proactive	Speak foreign languages

Describing your experience

I have five years' experience as a retailer/ teacher/ sales man.

I worked in trail for seven years and was promoted to manager in my second year.

I worked for Huawei as an engineer.

I studied at Tsinghua University.

Describing your goals for the future

I'm looking to further my skills, as an engineer in your hospital/company.

I want to further my career in physiotherapy, in administration/ as an administrator, in retail/ as a branch manager.

I believe your company is an important player in industry.

I feel my skills set is a perfect fit for your team and I can contribute by...

Models for Reference

Question 1: What do you consider are your most significant weaknesses?

What is your biggest flaw?

Skill: Don't feel the need to reveal deep character flaws and say it as it will sound like a weakness and a reason not to hire you. What they want to know is if it will interfere with your work and whether or not you're working to improve. The best way to answer this question is to turn this question around and turn a weakness into a strength.

Answers: I pay close attention to details which does result in a higher quality of work and saves additional time down the road, though it does take more time up front and sometimes my colleagues and I have to work overtime.

I tend to be a bit too easy-going. When you're too nice, people perceive you as a bit of a pushover. Sometimes I can get a little frustrated with my fellow co-workers if they can't keep the small talk from becoming excessive.

Question 2: What do you consider are your most significant strengths?

Why are you the best person for this position?

Skills: Exude confidence and don't be afraid to stroke your own ego here. Focus on this position in this company. Talk about the job related strengths and your achievements: how your involvement solved problems, reduced expenses, saved or made the company money, saved time, trained users to show value to your prospective employer.

Answers: I have a solid background in Hotel Management, great problem solving abilities. I get things done with little direction and sometimes in a creative way.

I can work well with different types of people of varying personalities and levels. I am motivated, disciplined, and determined to get my job done with quality and efficiency. I meet deadlines and deliver what I promise.

Case Study

How can you present qualities you possess which make you fit for this position?

Useful Expressions

commute	opening position	dimension	interact
promotion	pay increase	seniority	compensation
client servicing	initiative	alternative investments	
returns	fit in	follow-up meeting	

Models for Reference

Practice with the expressions you have learned in this unit and refer to the Model Dialogue if necessary.

Model Dialogue

Bob: Thanks so much for coming in to see us today! I was very impressed with your resume. Oh, and I noticed that your last job was just a few blocks from here? You must like this area?

Susan: Thank you for seeing me. Yes, I worked right up on State Street. I find it a good area to work in and an easy commute for me.

Bob: So, it appears from your resume that both of your last two jobs have a lot of similarities with the position we have open?

Susan: Yes, they do. I feel very well prepared for this opening. I've had solid experience in all dimensions of the job.

Bob: How would this job seem to be different from your current situation?

Susan: While the job function is pretty similar, I think the company situation would be quite a bit different. In my present job, I need to strictly stay within the bounds of my job description. I can't really interact with people in other departments, for example, without going through my boss. But there are limits to what I can and can't do on the job.

Bob: Beyond the day-to-day client servicing, could you tell me about any particular initiatives of which you are particularly proud in your current position?

Susan: More than anyone else in my office, I have led my clients aggressively into alternative investments. This has not only led to slightly higher returns, but it has also tightened my relationship with them and built their trust with me.

Bob: Susan, I really like what I have heard. I think that your style could fit in exceptionally well and you could be very happy here. I'll be back to you shortly to set up some times for a follow-up meeting with some of my colleagues as well.

Susan: Sounds great. I have heard positive things about your firm.

Class Time for Topic-related Discussion

Suppose you are the director of HR Department. You are now interviewing with applicants for your company. Find partners to be the interviewees and make up mimic interview together.

Practice these general questions.

■　Tell me about yourself.

■　What kind of work do you want to do?

■　What are your weaknesses?

■　Why have you chosen this career (position, company)?

■　What makes you think you are qualified for this position?

■　Could you describe a difficult problem and how you dealt with it?

■　What salary do you expect?

■　What would you like to be doing 5 years from now?

Further Reading

Tips for job interview

When you are requested for interviews, congratulations! You are ever closer to your goal of obtaining one or more job offers. Learning some tips and etiquette in interview can further ensure you the job you have been searching for.

The first one is searching. Search information about the employer and company, so you are better prepared of the questions your interviewer will ask. Practice your responses to the typical job interview questions.

When you get ready for the upcoming interview, you need to pay attention to whether your interview attire is neat, tidy and appropriate for the type of company you are interviewing with. You also need to keep your accessories and jewelry to a minimum.

Don't forget to bring a nice portfolio with copies of your resume, a pen and paper for note taking included.

On the day of the interview, the very first thing to abide by is to be on time. Arrive about 15 minutes before your scheduled interview to complete additional paperwork and allow yourself time to get settled. Turn off your phone before you head into the interview.

During the interview, there are also some interview etiquettes to know, such as staying engaged in the cross-talking, maintaining eye contact, leaning forward slightly when talking to your interviewer, and making an active effort to listen effectively.

After the interview, remember to thank the interviewer(s). You can start the process while at the interview, thanking each person who interviewed you. Writing thank-you emails in person and notes shortly after the interview will also certainly leave a good impression to your interviewer(s).

Things not to Miss

1. Background information

IBM, the International Business Machines Corporation (IBM) is a global technology and innovation company, with headquarters in Armonk, New York, United States. IBM manufactures and markets computer hardware and software, and offers infrastructure, hosting and consulting services. It is the largest technology and consulting employer in the world, with more than 300,000 employees serving clients in 160 countries.

The company was founded in 1911 as the Computing Tabulating Recording Company (CTR), through a merger of the Tabulating Machine Company, the International Time Recording Company, and the Computing Scale Company. On January 9, 2014, IBM announced to establish a new department with the cost of one billion US dollars, which deals with Watson, the latest computer system in IBM.

2. Conversational skills
Talk skillfully in the interview

Talking in the interview differs from that with your friends, mostly because you are too nervous to say anything. To calm you down, interviewer(s) would usually start the interview with a small talk exchanged with you, which will help the interviewer gain an understanding of your personality and how you communicate with people.

This first question is the time to help the interviewer start to see why you're the best person for the job. Therefore, it's important to focus on stories and professional experiences rather than give a run-down of your entire background and your family story. In the following parts, there are still some tips to help you conduct a skillful talking.

First, stay positive. Focusing on positive or neutral topic and avoiding mentioning any negative news issues or controversial current events will cause the mood of the interview to maintain in a positive direction.

Second, when answering questions, do it in a clear way without elaboration or extra examples. But also, be thoroughly and completely by not straying far from the original questions asked.

Third, skip the slang. Speak professionally during your interview with complete sentences and no slang terms or colloquialisms. You don't need to use big words outside your normal vocabulary either.

Finally, to sound professional, you should also avoid "um." To realize it, you can practice conducting an interview-length conversation with a friend and focus on eliminating these words from your speech if this is something you tend to do when you're nervous or speaking in public.

NOTES

Unit 15   In the Office

Five-minute Activity

A newly recruited employee is going to meet his co-workers working in the same office with him for the first time. Work with some of your classmates to act out this first meeting.

Useful Words and Expressions

Good morning. May I introduce myself? My name's Collin King and I'm new here.	This is David, our new fellow.
	Let me introduce you to our chief editor Mrs. Green.
I'd like to welcome you to our company.	
I would like you to meet our new comer, Lucy Lee. She just graduated from Beijing University.	I don't know anyone here. You'll have to introduce me.
	I'm new here and I'm sure I'll need some help getting used to the office.
If you need anything, just ask. I'll do my best to help you out.	assistant, personnel manager, sales manager,
	chiefeditor, clerk, department, managing
I've been looking forward to meeting you.	director, secretary

Models for Reference

Model Dialogue 1

A: Hi there! My name's George Green. You're new around here, huh?
B: Yes. My name's Mike Benson. I just started a couple of days ago.
A: Well, if there's anything I can do for you, let me know.
B: Thanks, I appreciate that!

NOTES

Model Dialogue 2

A: Come on in, David. Let me introduce you to some of our team.

　　Hi, guys, this is David. He just graduated from Beijing University. He'll begin working with us today.

B: Good morning! My name is David King and I'm new here. I've been looking forward to meeting you guys.

A: David, I'd like you to meet Mr. Black, our sales manager.

C: Welcome, David. If you need anything, just ask. I'll do my best to help you out.

B: Thank you, sir!

Case Study

What should you know about office etiquette when you are at your workplace?

Useful Expressions

We have succeeded in securing our share of the market in Canada.	We anticipated getting queries, so we employed someone for the hotline.
Tim managed to put everybody in a foul mood.	We can't afford to risk losing more customers and contracts.
He always manages to calm them down.	You get what you pay for.
I'll only come if you succeed in persuading Jacob to come.	What's the point of that question?
He's so diplomatic and understanding.	That's a questionable thing.
We have to try to avoid making mistakes this time.	You have a point there.
	Don't be ridiculous!

Models for Reference

Practice with the expressions you have learned in this unit and refer to the Model Dialogue if necessary.

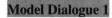

Model Dialogue 1

Turner: I'd like to thank you for taking the time to meet with me today. We have a lot of important things to discuss! We've managed to secure our share of the market in Canada and sales have continued to grow in the U.S., but what worries me is how things are progressing in Europe. Now，I'd like to discuss how we can succeed in increasing our market share in Europe.

Anna: I agree, but you have to bear in mind that we don't have a lot of experience in Europe.

Turner: You have a point there.

Anna: Quite frankly, you have to admit, that our products are the best on the market, and everyone knows that.

Turner: I think you're right, Anna. If we had greater exposure, we could expand our market share.

Carter: That's true to some extent, but there are other aspects to think about to avoid making mistakes.

Anna: I would like to emphasize taking the trouble to maintain a high level of service!

Carter: To be honest, we also need to assess our past performance.

Anna: Well, we can't postpone doing this until later. We simply can't afford to risk losing more customers and contracts.

Turner: Anna, don't be ridiculous. With talk like that, you'll manage to put everybody in a foul mood. You have to remember that we have succeeded in securing our share of the market in Canada.

Anna: I'd like to emphasize that we took the trouble to focus on customer needs in Canada and it really paid off.

Carter: I think we would be more effective if we centered our marketing efforts in Europe.

Turner: Well, this has proven to be a successful solution in Canada. If we could use a similar model, we should be able to increase our market share. You have to bear in mind, though, that Europe is not Canada! Things could get tricky!

Anna: I think we can succeed if we can manage to set up a marketing team in every individual country, and not have it all led by our offices here.

Carter: We really should emphasize putting someone on site. If we had a marketing team on location, we would be more responsive to our customer needs.

Anna: Yes, we currently only have one marketing office covering all of Europe. And that office is based here in Los Angeles. And I just don't think that it's effective.

Turner: I think we have a lot to gain by expanding our European marketing operation.

Anna: But wouldn't that cost a lot?

Carter: Well, maybe. It might entail reducing the size of the American office to cut costs. Considering the travel costs involved, this could be a viable option.

Turner: A complete cost analysis is necessary before making a final decision.

Anna: I'm afraid this won't be enough. Maybe we should also consider expanding the product line. Currently, we're only selling our most popular products in Europe.

Turner: That's true. Market research has shown that there is a lot of opportunity for specialized products in Europe.

Carter: And if we had a marketing team in Europe we would be able to tailor our products to our customers' needs.

Anna: Yes, I think by introducing a broader product line, combined with establishing a marketing team based in Europe, we could turn things around.

Turner: Yes, I think we should weigh the possibilities.

Carter: Anna, why don't you organize a team to do some research to see if this is worthwhile?

Anna: I'll get started on that right away.

Turner: Great! I think this meeting was really worthwhile. We have come up with some excellent proposals and I'm looking forward to seeing your report.

Model Dialogue 2

Susan: Hi! Jennifer! Can you help me with the minutes of the last meeting? Mike made a mess of them. Again!

Jennifer: Sure! Let me take a look.

Susan: I'm really fed up with Mike! He always makes careless mistakes, and it is really painful to work with him.

Jennifer: Come on! You shouldn't think like that. You'll always have some co-workers that are a little bit harder to work with than others. But if you are so negative in the office, there will be a bad working environment for everybody.

Susan: You are lucky that you don't have to work with him. The people in your department seem so capable and nice to be around. Say, Linda. She's so brilliant

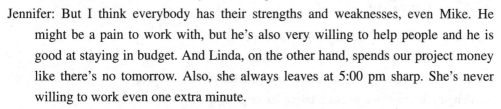

and radiant. I've never met anyone as delightful as she is.

Jennifer: But I think everybody has their strengths and weaknesses, even Mike. He might be a pain to work with, but he's also very willing to help people and he is good at staying in budget. And Linda, on the other hand, spends our project money like there's no tomorrow. Also, she always leaves at 5:00 pm sharp. She's never willing to work even one extra minute.

Susan: Do we have a perfect co-worker? What about Ben? Everybody loves him. Even though he's fresh out the college and still a bit green, he seems to be a great co-worker.

Jennifer: I think you're right. He's hard-working, easy to get along with, honest, and he never steals the credit on anything. The only thing he lacks is experience.

Susan: Maybe that's why he's so nice!

Class Time for Topic-related Discussion

Look at the following companies and think of areas in which cost savings could be made. Remember that reducing advertising or research and development expenditure could damage sales.

A well-known fast-food chain wants to improve its margins. It has targeted material costs as the simplest area to make savings.

An American car maker's manufacturing costs are too high, making its cars uncompetitive in the market.

Practice these key sentences.

- Money doesn't grow on trees.
- We have to try to avoid making mistakes this time.
- We have other priorities at the moment.
- Can we postpone doing this till next month?
- Do you remember talking about this at the last meeting?
- I recommend changing the whole concept.
- The plan entails demolishing the old shopping center.

Further Reading

The what and how of management innovation

Over the past century, breakthroughs such as brand management and the divisionalized organization structure have created more sustained competitive advantage than anything that came out of a lab or focus group.

What is management innovation?

A management innovation can be defined as a marked departure from traditional management principles, processes, and practices or a departure from customary organizational forms that significantly alters the way the work of management is performed. Put simply, management innovation changes how managers do what they do. And what do managers do? Typically, managerial work includes

- Setting goals and laying out plans;
- Motivating and aligning effort;
- Coordinating and controlling activities;
- Accumulating and allocating resources;
- Acquiring and applying knowledge;
- Building and nurturing relationships;
- Identifying and developing talent;
- Understanding and balancing the demands of outside constituencies.

In a big organization, the only way to change how managers work is to reinvent the processes that govern that work. Management processes such as strategic planning, capital budgeting, project management, hiring and promotion, employee assessment, executive development, internal communications, and knowledge management are the gears that turn management principles into everyday practices. They establish the recipes and rituals that govern the work of managers. While operational innovation focuses on a company's business processes (procurement, logistics, customer support, and so on), management innovation targets a company's management processes.

How to become a management innovator

If a senior executive claims that his or her company has a praiseworthy process for management innovation, what's missing, it seems, is a practical methodology. As with other types of innovation, the biggest challenge is generating truly novel ideas. While there is no sausage crank for innovation, it's possible to increase the odds of a "Eureka!"

moment by assembling the right ingredients. Some of the essential components are:

- A bewitching problem that demands fresh thinking;
- Novel principles or paradigms that have the power to illuminate new approaches;
- A careful deconstruction of the conventions and dogma that constrain creative thinking;
- Examples and analogies that help redefine what's possible.

Chunky problems. Fresh principles. Unorthodox thinking. Wisdom from the fringe. These multipliers of human creativity are as pivotal to management innovation as they are to every other kind of innovation.

It takes fortitude and perseverance, as well as imagination, to solve big problems. These qualities are most abundant when a problem is not only important but also inspiring. Frederick Winslow Taylor, arguably the most important management innovator of the twentieth century, is usually portrayed as a hard-nosed engineer, intent on mechanizing work and pushing employees to the max. Stern he may have been, but Taylor's single-minded devotion to efficiency stemmed from his conviction that it was iniquitous to waste an hour of human labor when a task could be redesigned to be performed with less effort.

Things not to Miss

1. Background information

Market share is the percentage of a market (defined in terms of either units or revenue) accounted for by a specific entity. Increasing market share is one of the most important objectives of business. The main advantage of using market share as a measure of business performance is that it is less dependent upon macroenvironmental variables such as the state of the economy or changes in tax policy. However, increasing market share may be dangerous for makers of fungible hazardous products, particularly products sold into the United States market, where they may be subject to market share liability.

Public relations (PR) is the practice of managing the spread of information between an individual or an organization(such as a business, a government agency, or a nonprofit organization) and the public. Public relations may include an organization or individual gaining exposure to their audiences using topics of public interest and news items that do not require direct payment. This differentiates it from advertising as a form of marketing communications. The aim of public relations is to inform the public, prospective customers, investors, partners, employees, and other stakeholders and ultimately persuade them to maintain a certain view about the organization, its leadership, products, or of political decisions. Public relations professionals typically work for PR and marketing firms, businesses and companies, government, government agencies, and public officials as PIOs, and nongovernmental organizations and nonprofit organizations.

2. Conversational skills
What to say when you don't know the answer

Although honesty is the only policy, however, blatantly admitting, "I don't know", in response to a direct question can be disastrous. The only solution is to be honest and maintain credibility at the same time. Keep in your back pocket the following strategies so that you can field even the toughest questions with credibility and confidence.

1) Reflection

Repeat the question and toss it back to your audience, "Does anyone here have any experience with that?" After you have fielded all of the contributions, be sure to summarize and add your own ideas if any have been sparked by the interaction.

2) I'll get back to you

This is an old standard and it works well if you do three things. First, write the question down. Second, tell the questioner exactly when you will get back to them. Third, be sure to get the questioner's contact information if you don't have it.

3) Defer to the expert

Combine the two techniques above when a question is legitimately outside of your area of expertise. If there is an expert present, ask him/her this question "Do you have any insights into that?" Otherwise, state that you will confer with an expert and get back to them.

4) Compliment the questioner

A sincere compliment always works well with the audience. "That's a great question. I've never thought about it that way. Does anyone here have any ideas on that?" Combined with other techniques, it will be quite effective.

5) Answer a question with a question

Sometimes questions are too narrow or too general to answer. Reserve the right, as the expert, to open a question up or close it down by asking a question in response. Instead of confessing "I don't know," you can ask a more enlightening question.

6) Parallel answer

If you don't know the bull's eye answer to a question, offer what you do know quickly to demonstrate some credibility and then combine with a previous technique. "I know that is possible in Excel. I'm not sure if that is available in PowerPoint. I'll research it at the break and get back to you." Refrain from droning on and on about your parallel knowledge.

Unit 16   Advertisement

Five-minute Activity

Step One: Grab something around you randomly, like a cell phone, a textbook, a pair of glasses, an iPad...

Step Two: Suppose you are working for an advertising company, and try to come up with a great idea to advertise your "product" (the cell phone, the textbook, the pair of glasses, the iPad...)

Useful Expressions

Tips on how to create an ad

Understand your audience and identify your target customers.
Identify the competition.
Describe the current market.
Develop a strategy.
Come up with a snappy tagline.
Find a way to connect the desire of customers to what you are advertising.
Make sure all the relevant information is included.
Decide where and when to advertise.
Choose a memorable image.
Distinguish yourself from your top competitor.

Criteria for good ads

Memorable and easily recalled
Connects with audience
Provides information quickly and concisely

Doesn't confuse the viewer

Make the viewer willing to hunt for the pertinent information

Calls the viewer to action

Strong visuals

Models for Reference

Some famous advertising slogans:

Just do it. (Nike)

The sign of excellence. (Omega)

Quality never goes out of style. (Levis)

Engineered to move the human spirit. (Mercedes-Benz)

The good things in life never change. (Burberry)

Live your dream. (AnnaSui)

Cool Water. (Davidoff)

Every woman alive wants Chanel No.5. (Chanel No.5)

Case Study

How many different types of ad do you know? Share the most impressive ad with us.

Useful Expressions

A national campaign will start next month.	There are advertisements everywhere here in the city.
I think we can also run billboard and print ads to help create board brand recognition.	I like all the different colors and I like the billboards with eye-catching pictures and slogans.
Steven, have you got any ideas about the advertising of our new product?	I think that companies spend far too much money on advertising.
What kind of music are you going to have in the background?	If companies don't spend money on advertising, no one would hear about their products.
We could take out some advertisements to local newspapers.	Newspapers, magazines, television, and the

Let's get to work on our advertising campaign. Clever advertisements are just temptation to spend money. There is too much advertising gimmickry.	Internet are important media for advertising. Many others think advertisements are very unpleasant.

Models for Reference

Practice with the expressions you have learned in this unit and refer to the Model Dialogue if necessary.

Model Dialogue 1

Tina: Hi! Caroline. How are you today?

Caroline: I'm doing fine. How about you?

Tina: Great, thanks. So, how is our advertising campaign coming along?

Caroline: As I mentioned to you on the phone yesterday, a national campaign will start next month. We've decided to use a variety of media for full coverage. First, we'll do 15-second radio commercials 3 times a day in some big cities. At the same time, we'll have 30-second spots on television once a day for 3 weeks. Finally, we'll have some outdoor ads using billboards near the main entrances to big cities.

Tina: What style will the ads be?

Caroline: We're focusing on slice of life, showing how you can beat the summer heat by biting into a cool ice-cream sandwich. We'll also show everyone there are variety of flavors and they're not stuck with just strawberry.

Tina: Sounds like a brilliant idea. Will we have a new slogan?

Caroline: Definitely. The advertising agency's working on that right now. They'll have some proposals ready by the end of the day.

Tina: Sounds like we'll have a winner on our hands!

Model Dialogue 2

Agent: This Victorian style house was built in 1875. Many houses like this can be seen all over New Orleans and especially in the Garden District.

Jimmy: Wow. I really like the big windows and that Fancy wooden door!

Agent: Yes, this house is the oldest in the neighborhood too, and it's one of my favorites. You're really lucky that it's for sale! You know, these houses were built to last. They've survived floods, hurricanes…

Jimmy: I can imagine! Why would anyone want to sell such a beautiful old house?

Agent: Well, the owner doesn't have any family. The extra rooms are rented out to students now, but she's old and she wants to lead a quiet life. Apparently, the students don't help the landlady at all with the housework. The laundry piles up in the hallway, dishes are left in the sink and the floor is never swept. A complete mess!

Jimmy: Well, I don't mind a little dust, as long as the house is kept in good condition. Does the house have a garage and a basement?

Agent: Well, it's hard to see the garage from here, but it's behind the porch, next to the stairs. The basement was converted into another bedroom.

Jimmy: Oh great, so that room could be rented out! Can we take a closer look? Well, this doesn't look good here! What are these holes in the porch? I hope the house isn't being eaten by termite!

Agent: No, no, no, there are no termites, but the house does need to be worked on.

Jimmy: Yes, I can see that the house hasn't been worked on for years. It could really use a fresh coat of paint!

Agent: Yeah, the wood here on the porch is in bad shape and the house does need to be painted, but the walls and windows are in good shape, don't you think?

Jimmy: Oh, yes. And I just love these old crystal windows! You don't see them very often these days.

Agent: They just need to be washed.

Jimmy: I really like that big balcony, too! Just imagine having a nice Sunday brunch up there.

Agent: Oh, yes, you could spend the whole day up there relaxing and reading a book! And in the winter you could sit by the fireplace. Do you see the chimney up there on the roof? I'm sure it just needs to be swept.

Jimmy: The rooms get a lot of sun, don't they? I can't imagine that they need to be heated much. Do the rooms upstairs have fireplaces too?

Agent: The master bedroom upstairs has one, but the other rooms don't, so ... what do you think? Do you want to make an offer?

Jimmy: I really like this house a lot, even though it needs to be worked on. I mean, it has such a long history. A real survivor! Yes, I want it. Where there's a will, there's a way!

Class Time for Topic-related Discussion

You work for a cosmetics company and your company has recently launched a new product. Now you are supposed to persuade the editor of a fashion magazine who has a long-standing business cooperation relationship with you to give you a larger ad space.

Practice these key sentences.
- A signed photograph will be given away as a gimmick.
- Considering the work that was involved, I think it was worth the risk.
- We need more space to present our new product line.
- We are promoting brand awareness in China.
- The brand awareness developed by our company is tremendous.
- Customers desiring a free sample of our product should call our toll-free number.
- There are many insertions of advertisement in the newspapers.
- We will be asking that famous basketball player to endorse our product.

Further Reading

Product advertising

Product advertising is the art of building and maintaining product awareness with potential buyers. It is any method of communication about the promotion of a product in an attempt to induce prospective customers to purchase the product. In most cases the goal of product advertising is to clearly promote a specific product to a targeted audience by demonstrating differences between the product and competing products.

Before an advertisement idea is created, market research is usually conducted to obtain information such as consumers' needs, factors or people that influence purchasing decisions, and the types of media via which consumers can obtain product information.

The collected data is then used to write an advertisement plan and to determine how the message will be channeled to potential customers.

A successful advertising program informs potential customers about why they need the product, how it is used and the benefits the customer can get. A good advertisement also tells the consumer how the product is better than competing products that are also available on the market.

Within the general category of product advertising are several subtypes. They are primary advertising, selective advertising, mass advertising, class advertising, and cooperative advertising. Primary advertising aims at stimulating an interest in and a desire for a certain class of goods. Frequently the goods are some new type of product that has just come on the market or an established product that is seeking to expand its market. Selective advertising is intended to direct consumers toward the purchase of a particular brand of goods. Mass advertising is supposed to appeal to a cross section of people. Class advertising is directed at certain groups of people, such as college students or industrial purchasing agents. Cooperative advertising is a form of product advertising where the costs of advertising are shared by manufacturers and their middlemen.

Things not to Miss

1. Background information
What are pop-up ads?

Pop-up ads are advertisements that show up in a new browser window that appears out of nowhere as you are viewing content on the web. There's no one standard size for pop-up ads. Pop-up ads also vary widely in the amount of browser commands that show in the window and they are just one form of internet advertising used by advertisers to get web users' attention.

Besides, there are also pop-unders, which display windows behind your web browser window. Although they are generated by the same type of programming, some consider them different as pop-unders do not appear to be so intrusive. However, when you consider the level of annoyance, pop-ups and pop-unders are basically the same.

Among the other types of ads are ads that appear when you're clicking from one page to another (interstitials), ads located within a page you're reading, ads that appear when you've searched for a keyword or term, ads that are highly animated or appear as interactive games, ads that appear like stand alone websites, ads that appear in e-mail, branded sites or sponsored web pages and many others, etc. The only limit really is the ever changing online media technology and that's not much of a limit at all. Pop-up ads are just one of the various methods in reaching online consumers.

2. Conversational skills

Have a conversation with a celebrity

Have you ever met a celebrity, for example, a movie star, a sports star or the CEO of an international corporation? In case you would one day, you should know how to speak with one.

What follows shows good manners and ways to have while meeting a celebrity, like Jackie Chan or Obama.

Introduce yourself. The celebrity won't want to sign an autograph that says, "Dear Anonymous, keep living your dreams—hugs and kisses, the celebrity."

Don't go crazy and keep screaming their name. Say "Thank you, I am your biggest fan!" and compliment them on their show or their recent work. This doesn't mean being sophisticated and boring. It just means being polite. Be yourself, but you should start out on the right foot manners.

Never be afraid to tell them your opinions about their work. Be polite, but they know that not everyone likes every performance or every new product.

Ask about their plans. They love to talk about upcoming auditions, parties, new products, new policies and new decisions to anyone who would love to listen.

Although they are famous people, remember that they are just regular people on the inside. It's okay to get an autograph, a handshake or even a hug, but don't go nuts on them. It looks so much more sophisticated when you treat them like a friend. They will also have higher respect for you and talk more with you for not melting in their hands. Even though they are celebrities, don't make it all about them. Maybe being tired of being talked about all the time, they want to hear about you, too. When the person you are meeting asks "What's your favorite food"? or any other question, answer with a complete sentence, "My favorite food is pizza. What's yours?" instead of "Pizza". This is a more polite way of doing things.

Take a picture. No matter how happy or excited you are, don't use a scary grin. A sweet, natural smile would just be fine!